Contents

Discover the Magic of Taekwondo Patterns!

Join Sam on an Extraordinary Journey Through History and Taekwondo!

Are you ready to embark on a magical adventure? Dive into the pages of our enchanting book and follow Sam, a young Taekwondo student, as he uncovers the secrets behind the ancient patterns of this martial art. Perfect for children learning Taekwondo, this book is filled with exciting stories, historical insights, and valuable lessons that bring each Taekwondo pattern to life.

What's Inside?

- Magical Adventures: Travel with Sam as he is transported to different historical eras, meeting legendary figures and witnessing pivotal events that shaped the essence of Taekwondo.

- Historical Legends: Learn about the inspiring stories of figures like Dan Gun, the founder of Korea, and General Yi Sun-sin, a hero of Korean history, and many more!

- Meaningful Lessons: Discover the deep meanings behind each pattern, such as resilience, wisdom, unity, and the pursuit of peace, and how these values are woven into the fabric of Taekwondo.

Why This Book

- Educational: Provides a rich understanding of Taekwondo's history and philosophy, enhancing your child's appreciation and knowledge of the martial art.

- Inspiring: Teaches valuable life lessons and virtues that are central to Taekwondo and essential for personal growth.

- Entertaining: Combines adventure and learning in a way that keeps children engaged and excited to turn each page.

Perfect For:

- Taekwondo Students: Enhance your training with deeper insights into the patterns and their meanings.

- Young Historians: Explore fascinating historical stories and learn about important cultural figures.

- Curious Minds: Ignite a passion for learning with a blend of magic, history, and martial arts.

Join Sam on this unforgettable journey and discover the true spirit of Taekwondo. This book is not just about learning a martial art—it's about embracing values that will guide you throughout your life.

Order your copy today and step into the world of Taekwondo like never before!

Unlock the mysteries of Taekwondo patterns and let your journey begin!

Disclaimer

While this book is based on historical events and figures, some elements have been adapted or fictionalised for storytelling purposes. The characters, adventures, and interpretations of historical events are intended to inspire and educate young readers about the values and principles of Taekwondo. Although efforts have been made to ensure the historical accuracy of the content, certain details may have been simplified or altered to enhance the narrative and readability for children. For a more comprehensive understanding of Korean history and Taekwondo, we encourage readers to consult additional resources and engage in further study.

About the Spelling and Terms in This Book

In this book, we use "Taekwondo" rather than "Taekwon-do" for simplicity and readability. Both spellings refer to the same martial art.

You might also notice variations in the spelling of some Korean words and names. This happens because Korean words are transliterated into the Roman alphabet, and there are several accepted systems for doing so. For example, you might see "Dan Gun" spelled as "Dangun" or "Yul Gok" as "Yulgok."

These differences in spelling do not change the historical significance or the principles being taught. Our goal is to introduce you to the rich history and philosophy of Taekwondo in an engaging and accessible way. If you continue your Taekwondo journey, you may encounter different spellings and terms, but remember that the core values and lessons remain constant.

Happy reading and learning!

Chapter 1: The Journey Begins with Chon Ji

Means literally the "Heaven the Earth." It is, in the Orient, interpreted as the creation of the world or the beginning of human history, therefore, it is the initial pattern played by the beginner. This pattern consists of two similar parts, one to represent the Heaven, one to represent the Earth.

19 Movements

The dojang was buzzing with energy as Sam stepped inside for the very first time. He felt a mix of excitement and nerves bubbling inside him. At thirteen, he was eager to start his Taekwondo journey, a path he hoped would teach him discipline, strength, and focus. The walls of the training hall were adorned with various martial arts weapons and equipment, each piece holding its own story and purpose.

As the class began, Sam stood in line with the other beginners, listening intently to Master Lee, a seasoned Taekwondo instructor with decades of experience. Master Lee's voice was calm yet commanding, drawing everyone's attention effortlessly.

"Welcome, students. Today, we embark on a journey of self-discovery and discipline. Taekwondo is not just about physical strength but also about the strength of character and spirit. We begin with the basics. Sam, could you please fetch a pair of focus mitts from the equipment cupboard?"

Sam nodded and hurried towards the cupboard at the back of the dojang. As he opened the door, he was greeted by an array of neatly arranged equipment. He scanned the shelves for the mitts but something else caught his eye. Lying on the floor, partially hidden under a shelf, was an old, weathered belt. It looked out of place, almost forgotten.

Curiosity piqued, Sam bent down and picked it up. The moment his fingers touched the fabric, a strange sensation washed over him. The room seemed to spin, and he felt a sudden rush of wind. Before he could react, everything went dark.

When Sam opened his eyes, he found himself standing on the edge of a serene, crystal-clear lake. The air was cool and fresh, filled with the scent of pine and earth. He looked around in amazement, recognizing the place from the pictures he had seen in books. It was Lake Chon Ji, the legendary lake at the top of Mount Paektu, known as the meeting place of heaven and earth in Korean mythology.

As he marvelled at the beauty of the lake, a figure emerged from the mist. An old man, dressed in traditional Korean hanbok, approached him with a kind smile.

"Welcome, young one," the old man said. "You have been brought here to learn the true meaning of Chon Ji, the first pattern of Taekwondo. It signifies the creation of the world, where heaven and earth meet in perfect harmony. This place is sacred, a symbol of the balance and unity that we strive for in our practice."

Sam listened in awe as the old man continued. "In ancient times, this lake was considered the cradle of civilization. It was here that the Korean people believed heaven and earth came together to create life. The pattern Chon Ji reflects this balance, teaching us the importance of harmony between mind, body, and spirit."

As the old man spoke, Sam felt a profound connection to the place and the story. He realized that Taekwondo was more than just physical training; it was a journey into history and philosophy, a way to understand the deeper meanings behind each movement and pattern.

The old man handed Sam the ancient belt he had found in the dojang. "This belt is a key, a bridge between your world and the world of Taekwondo's history. Each time you find yourself here, you will learn about the patterns and the stories they hold. Remember, young one, the true strength of Taekwondo lies not in the power of your kicks or punches, but in the wisdom and balance you cultivate within."

With those words, the old man began to fade, and the surroundings blurred once more. Sam felt himself being pulled back, the world spinning around him. When he opened his eyes again, he was back in the dojang, clutching the old belt in his hand.

Master Lee's voice brought him back to reality. "Sam, did you find the mitts?"

Startled, Sam quickly grabbed the mitts from the shelf and returned to the group. As he handed them to Master Lee, he couldn't help but feel a sense of awe and wonder. He knew that his Taekwondo journey was going to be much more than he had ever imagined.

As the class continued, Sam's mind kept drifting back to the serene waters of Lake Chon Ji and the wise words of the old man. He understood now that every pattern he would learn had a story, a history that connected him to something greater. And with each lesson, he would unlock more of the ancient wisdom hidden within the art of Taekwondo.

Chapter 2: The Legend of Dan Gun

---

*Dan Gun is named after the Holy Dan-Gun,
the legendary founder of Korea in the year
2333 BC.*

21 Movements

The next few days flew by in a blur of schoolwork and
anticipation. Sam couldn't stop thinking about his incredible
experience at Lake Chon Ji and the old man's words. He was
eager for his next Taekwondo lesson, curious to see if he would
again be transported to another world of history and legend.

When Saturday finally arrived, Sam made his way to the dojang
with a spring in his step. The training hall was just as bustling as
before, filled with students of all ages practicing their kicks,
punches, and forms. Master Lee greeted him with a knowing
smile, as if he sensed Sam's newfound eagerness.

"Good to see you again, Sam," Master Lee said. "Today, we will
begin learning the second pattern, Dan Gun. This pattern is
named after the legendary founder of Korea. Are you ready?"

Sam nodded enthusiastically, and the class began with warm-
up exercises and basic drills. Master Lee then demonstrated
the Dan Gun pattern, each movement precise and purposeful.

Sam followed along, doing his best to mimic the master's fluid motions.

After class, Master Lee called Sam aside. "I need you to help me with something in the storage room," he said. Sam's heart raced with excitement as he followed Master Lee to the back of the dojang. They entered a small, dimly lit room filled with various pieces of equipment and training gear.

"Look around and find the wooden sword," Master Lee instructed. Sam began searching through the room, his eyes scanning the shelves and corners. As he moved a stack of mats, he noticed something glimmering in the shadows. It was the same ancient belt he had found before, lying on the floor as if waiting for him.

With a sense of déjà vu, Sam picked up the belt. Instantly, he felt the now-familiar rush of wind and darkness enveloped him. When he opened his eyes, he found himself standing in a vast, verdant valley. The landscape was breathtaking, with rolling hills, lush forests, and clear blue skies stretching as far as the eye could see.

"Welcome, Sam," a voice called out. Sam turned to see the old man from Lake Chon Ji standing nearby, his wise eyes twinkling with warmth.

"Where am I?" Sam asked, marvelling at the beauty around him.

"This is the ancient land of Gojoseon, the first Korean kingdom," the old man explained. "You are here to learn about Dan Gun, the legendary founder of Korea. According to the myth, Dan Gun was the son of Hwanung, a heavenly prince, and a bear who transformed into a woman. He established the kingdom of Gojoseon in 2333 BCE, bringing order and civilization to the people."

As the old man spoke, the scenery around them began to shift. Sam found himself standing in a bustling ancient city. He saw people building homes, tending to crops, and engaging in various crafts. The air was filled with the sounds of hammers, voices, and laughter.

"Dan Gun is a symbol of Korea's origin and identity," the old man continued. "He represents the unity of heaven and earth, much like the pattern Chon Ji you learned about before. Through his leadership, he taught his people agriculture, law, and the arts, laying the foundation for Korean culture and society."

Sam watched in awe as a grand procession approached. At its centre was a tall, regal figure dressed in elaborate robes, with a crown that shimmered in the sunlight. The people bowed respectfully as he passed, their faces filled with admiration and reverence.

"That is Dan Gun," the old man said. "He was not just a king, but a wise and just leader who guided his people with compassion and wisdom. The pattern Dan Gun in Taekwondo honours his legacy and the values he stood for—leadership, wisdom, and the pursuit of harmony."

As Sam absorbed the story, he felt a deep sense of connection to the ancient legend. He understood now that each Taekwondo pattern was more than just a series of movements; it was a tribute to the rich history and cultural heritage of Korea.

The old man placed a hand on Sam's shoulder. "Remember, Sam, the true essence of Taekwondo lies not just in physical prowess but in understanding and embodying the principles behind each pattern. Dan Gun's story teaches us the importance of wisdom, leadership, and the unification of heaven and earth within ourselves."

Once again, the world around Sam began to blur. He felt the familiar sensation of being pulled back, and when he opened his eyes, he was back in the storage room of the dojang, holding the ancient belt.

"Did you find the sword?" Master Lee's voice broke through his thoughts. Sam quickly spotted the wooden sword on a nearby shelf and handed it to the master.

"Thank you, Sam," Master Lee said with a nod. "You seem more focused today. Keep that spirit, and you'll progress well in your training."

As Sam left the dojang, he couldn't help but smile. He knew that his Taekwondo journey was not just about learning techniques and patterns but also about discovering the deeper meanings and stories that lay within each one. With every lesson, he would continue to unlock the ancient wisdom of Taekwondo, guided by the legends and history of Korea.

Chapter 3: The Legacy of Do San

Do San is the pseudonym of the patriot Ahn Chang-Ho (1876-1938). The 24 movements represent his entire life which he devoted to furthering the education of Korea and its independence movement.

24 Movements

The days following his encounter with Dan Gun's legend were filled with an unquenchable curiosity for the deeper meanings behind each Taekwondo pattern. Sam found himself eagerly anticipating his next lesson, wondering what new adventure awaited him. As he walked into the dojang on a crisp Thursday evening, the familiar buzz of activity greeted him. Students were warming up, their movements a symphony of discipline and energy.

Master Lee stood at the front, exuding his usual calm authority. "Today, we will move on to the next pattern in our journey: Do San," he announced, his voice carrying across the room. "Do San represents Ahn Chang-Ho, a prominent Korean independence activist and educator. His contributions to the Korean independence movement are immense, and his life is a testament to perseverance and dedication."

Sam listened intently, his mind already racing with questions about this new historical figure. As the class progressed, Master

Lee demonstrated the Do San pattern, each movement imbued with a sense of purpose and history. Sam tried to absorb every detail, feeling the weight of the legacy in each motion.

After class, as the students began to disperse, Master Lee approached Sam. "Sam, could you help me fetch a training manual from the archive room? It's on the top shelf, in the corner."

Sam nodded eagerly, suspecting another journey awaited him. He made his way to the archive room, a small space filled with shelves of books, manuals, and old training equipment. As he searched for the manual, his eyes fell upon the now-familiar ancient belt, neatly folded on a high shelf. Without hesitation, he reached for it.

The moment his fingers brushed the fabric, the world around him dissolved into a swirl of colours. When the spinning stopped, Sam found himself standing in a bustling city street, the architecture distinctly early 20th century. The streets were alive with people going about their daily lives, but there was an underlying tension in the air.

"Welcome, Sam," the old man's voice greeted him. Turning, Sam saw his wise guide from the previous journeys, standing beside him in the bustling cityscape.

"Where are we now?" Sam asked, taking in the unfamiliar surroundings.

"This is Seoul, during the early 1900s," the old man explained. "You are here to learn about Do San, the pen name of Ahn Chang-Ho, a key figure in Korea's struggle for independence from Japanese occupation. Ahn Chang-Ho was not only a freedom fighter but also an educator and a leader who inspired many through his vision and unwavering commitment to his people."

As the old man spoke, the scene shifted, and Sam found himself in a modest classroom. A group of children sat attentively, listening to a passionate young man at the front of the room. His eyes sparkled with intelligence and determination as he spoke about the importance of education and national pride.

"That is Ahn Chang-Ho," the old man said. "He believed that the path to independence was through education and the cultivation of strong moral character. He founded schools and organizations to promote these ideals, emphasizing the need for self-improvement and unity among Koreans."

Sam watched as Ahn Chang-Ho moved among the children, encouraging them with kind words and a gentle smile. The respect and admiration in their eyes were evident, a testament to his influence and charisma.

The scene changed again, and Sam found himself in a crowded hall where Ahn Chang-Ho addressed a large gathering of adults.

His voice was firm and resolute as he spoke about the struggle for independence, the need for perseverance, and the hope for a brighter future.

"Ahn Chang-Ho's efforts extended beyond education," the old man continued. "He was instrumental in forming the Korean National Association and other groups that sought to unite Koreans in their fight against oppression. His pseudonym, Do San, means 'Island Mountain,' symbolizing his steadfast and unyielding nature."

As Sam absorbed these lessons, he felt a deep respect for Ahn Chang-Ho's legacy. He realized that the pattern Do San in Taekwondo was more than a series of movements; it was a tribute to a man who dedicated his life to the betterment of his people, embodying the principles of perseverance, integrity, and selflessness.

The old man turned to Sam with a serious expression. "Do San teaches us that true strength lies not only in physical prowess but in the courage to stand up for what is right, the wisdom to educate and inspire others, and the dedication to a cause greater than oneself."

The world around Sam began to blur once more, and he felt the familiar pull back to the present. When he opened his eyes, he was back in the archive room, the ancient belt still in his hand.

Master Lee's voice called out from the doorway. "Did you find the manual, Sam?"

Quickly, Sam located the manual on the top shelf and handed it to Master Lee. "Thank you, Sam. You seem more focused and determined with each passing day."

As Sam left the dojang, he felt a profound sense of purpose. He understood now that each Taekwondo pattern was a bridge to the past, a way to connect with the values and principles of those who came before him. With every lesson, he was not only learning the art of Taekwondo but also the rich history and enduring spirit of Korea.

Walking home, Sam felt a renewed sense of determination. He was eager to continue his journey, to learn more about the legends and heroes behind each pattern, and to embody the values they represented in his own life.

Chapter 4: The Enlightenment of Won Hyo

Won Hyo was the noted monk who introduced Buddhism to the Silla Dynasty in the year of 686 AD.

28 Movements

The dojang was bathed in the soft glow of the afternoon sun as Sam arrived for his next lesson. His mind buzzed with the stories of Ahn Chang-Ho and Dan Gun, and he was eager to discover what new history awaited him. He entered the training hall with a sense of purpose, his steps confident and his heart open to the lessons ahead.

Master Lee greeted the students with his usual composed demeanour. "Today, we will learn about the fourth pattern: Won Hyo. This pattern is named after the renowned monk Won Hyo, who played a significant role in the spread of Buddhism in Korea. His life and teachings have left a lasting impact on Korean culture and philosophy."

Sam watched intently as Master Lee demonstrated the intricate movements of the Won Hyo pattern. Each step and strike seemed to flow with a sense of spiritual grace, reflecting the inner peace and enlightenment that Won Hyo sought to bring to others.

After class, as the other students began to pack up, Master Lee approached Sam. "Sam, could you help me retrieve a meditation cushion from the supply room? It's the large, green one in the corner."

Sam nodded, his excitement building. He headed to the supply room, a small space filled with various items neatly stacked on shelves. As he searched for the cushion, his eyes caught sight of the ancient belt once more, resting on a high shelf. He reached for it, feeling the now-familiar rush of anticipation.

The moment his fingers touched the belt, the world around him dissolved into a swirl of colours. When the spinning stopped, Sam found himself standing in a serene temple courtyard. The air was filled with the sound of rustling leaves and the gentle hum of chanting monks. The atmosphere was peaceful, inviting contemplation and reflection.

"Welcome, Sam," the old man's voice greeted him. Sam turned to see his wise guide standing beside him, a calm smile on his face.

"Where are we now?" Sam asked, taking in the tranquil surroundings.

"This is the temple of Bulguksa, during the Silla Dynasty," the old man explained. "You are here to learn about Won Hyo, a legendary monk whose teachings and actions greatly influenced Korean Buddhism. Won Hyo's story is one of enlightenment and spiritual awakening."

As the old man spoke, the scene shifted, and Sam found himself in a modest room within the temple. A young monk sat in deep meditation, his face serene and focused. Sam recognized him from the descriptions he had read – this was Won Hyo, before his enlightenment.

"Won Hyo was a scholar and a seeker," the old man continued. "He studied Buddhist texts diligently, seeking enlightenment and understanding. However, it wasn't through study alone that he found his true path."

The scene changed again, and Sam saw Won Hyo traveling with another monk, their journey taking them through forests and mountains. One night, they sought shelter in a dark cave. As Won Hyo drank from a bowl of water he found in the cave, he experienced a profound moment of clarity. When morning came, he realized the cave was actually a tomb, and the water bowl was a human skull.

"That moment was Won Hyo's great awakening," the old man explained. "He realized that enlightenment came not from external rituals or objects, but from within. He abandoned his journey to China and returned to Korea, spreading the message that true enlightenment is found in one's mind and heart."

Sam watched as Won Hyo taught his followers, his words filled with compassion and wisdom. He emphasized the importance of understanding and kindness, teaching that enlightenment was accessible to everyone, regardless of their status or background.

"Won Hyo's teachings remind us of the importance of inner peace and self-awareness," the old man said. "The pattern Won Hyo in Taekwondo reflects this journey of enlightenment, encouraging us to seek balance and harmony within ourselves."

As Sam absorbed these lessons, he felt a deep sense of tranquillity. He realized that the essence of Won Hyo's teachings was not just about physical practice but about cultivating a peaceful and enlightened mind.

The old man placed a hand on Sam's shoulder. "Remember, Sam, the true strength of Taekwondo lies not only in mastering techniques but in understanding the spiritual and philosophical foundations behind them. Won Hyo's story teaches us that enlightenment and true power come from within."

The world around Sam began to blur once more, and he felt the familiar pull back to the present. When he opened his eyes, he was back in the supply room, the ancient belt still in his hand.

Master Lee's voice called out from the doorway. "Did you find the cushion, Sam?"

Quickly, Sam located the large, green meditation cushion and handed it to Master Lee. "Thank you, Sam. You seem more centred and calmer with each passing lesson."

As Sam left the dojang, he felt a profound sense of inner peace. He understood now that each Taekwondo pattern was not only a physical exercise but a journey into the depths of history and philosophy. With every lesson, he was not only learning the art of Taekwondo but also the wisdom and enlightenment that came with it.

Walking home, Sam felt a renewed sense of purpose. He was eager to continue his journey, to learn more about the legends and teachings behind each pattern, and to embody the values they represented in his own life. The story of Won Hyo had taught him that true strength and enlightenment came from within, a lesson he would carry with him both in and out of the dojang.

Chapter 5: The Wisdom of Yul Gok

Yul Gok is the pseudonym of a great philosopher and scholar Yi I (1536-1584) nicknamed the "Confucius of Korea". The 38 movements of this pattern refer to his birthplace on 38-degree latitude and the diagram represents "scholar".

38 Movements

The sun was beginning to set as Sam made his way to the dojang for his evening class. His heart beat with a mix of excitement and curiosity, eager to uncover the next chapter in his Taekwondo journey. The previous lessons had instilled in him a deep respect for the historical and philosophical foundations of Taekwondo, and he was ready to learn more.

As he entered the dojang, the familiar sounds of students training and the sight of Master Lee's calm, authoritative presence greeted him. "Gather around, everyone," Master Lee called out. "Tonight, we will explore the fifth pattern: Yul Gok. This pattern is named after Yi I, one of Korea's most revered Confucian scholars, who is also known by his pen name, Yul Gok. His contributions to Korean philosophy and education are profound and enduring."

Sam watched intently as Master Lee demonstrated the Yul Gok pattern, each movement reflecting the precision and intellectual depth of the scholar it was named after. The pattern was complex, demanding not just physical skill but also a keen understanding of its underlying principles.

After class, Master Lee approached Sam with a thoughtful expression. "Sam, could you help me find a scroll in the library? It's an old text on Confucian philosophy, stored in the back."

Sam nodded eagerly and made his way to the library, a quiet room filled with rows of ancient books and manuscripts. As he searched through the shelves, his eyes fell upon the ancient belt, once again lying on a high shelf. He reached for it, feeling the familiar thrill of anticipation.

The moment his fingers touched the belt, the world around him dissolved into a swirl of colours. When the spinning stopped, Sam found himself standing in a peaceful garden, surrounded by scholars dressed in traditional Korean hanbok. The air was filled with the scent of blooming flowers and the soft rustle of leaves.

"Welcome, Sam," the old man's voice greeted him. Turning, Sam saw his wise guide standing beside him, a gentle smile on his face.

"Where are we now?" Sam asked, taking in the serene surroundings.

"This is the village of Yulgok-ri during the Joseon Dynasty," the old man explained. "You are here to learn about Yi I, also known as Yul Gok, one of Korea's greatest Confucian scholars. His teachings and writings have had a lasting impact on Korean education, ethics, and governance."

As the old man spoke, the scene shifted, and Sam found himself in a modest study. A young scholar sat at a desk, diligently writing by the light of an oil lamp. Sam recognized him from the descriptions he had read—this was Yi I, deep in thought and surrounded by books and scrolls.

"Yi I was a prodigy," the old man continued. "He passed the highest civil service exam at the age of thirteen and went on to become a respected teacher and advisor to the court. He believed in the importance of education, moral integrity, and the cultivation of virtue."

The scene changed again, and Sam saw Yi I teaching a group of students in a courtyard. His voice was calm and authoritative as he explained the principles of Confucianism, emphasizing the importance of righteousness, filial piety, and the pursuit of knowledge.

"Yul Gok's teachings were grounded in Confucian ideals," the old man said. "He believed that a just and prosperous society could only be achieved through the cultivation of moral character and the proper education of its leaders. His works, such as the 'Ten Diagrams on Sage Learning,' provided a comprehensive guide to personal and governmental ethics."

As Sam absorbed these lessons, he felt a deep respect for Yi I's legacy. He realized that the pattern Yul Gok in Taekwondo was more than a series of movements; it was a tribute to a man who dedicated his life to the pursuit of knowledge and the betterment of society.

The old man placed a hand on Sam's shoulder. "Remember, Sam, the true strength of Taekwondo lies not only in physical prowess but in the wisdom and integrity you cultivate within yourself. Yul Gok's story teaches us the importance of education, moral character, and the pursuit of knowledge."

The world around Sam began to blur once more, and he felt the familiar pull back to the present. When he opened his eyes, he was back in the library, the ancient belt still in his hand.

Master Lee's voice called out from the doorway. "Did you find the scroll, Sam?"

Quickly, Sam located the scroll on Confucian philosophy and handed it to Master Lee. "Thank you, Sam. You seem to be gaining a deeper understanding of the patterns with each lesson."

As Sam left the dojang, he felt a profound sense of intellectual fulfilment. He understood now that each Taekwondo pattern was not only a physical exercise but a journey into the depths of history and philosophy. With every lesson, he was not only learning the art of Taekwondo but also the wisdom and enlightenment that came with it.

Walking home, Sam felt a renewed sense of purpose. He was eager to continue his journey, to learn more about the legends and teachings behind each pattern, and to embody the values they represented in his own life. The story of Yul Gok had taught him that true strength and enlightenment came from the pursuit of knowledge and the cultivation of moral character, lessons he would carry with him both in and out of the dojang.

Chapter 6: The Heroism of Joong Gun

Joong Gun is named after the patriot Ahn Joong-Gun who assassinated Hiro-Bumi Ito, the first Japanese governor-general of Korea, known as the man who played the leading part in the Korea- Japan merger. There are 32 movements in this pattern to represent Mr. Ahn's age when he was executed at Lui-Shung prison (1910).

32 Movements

The sun was setting, casting long shadows across the dojang as Sam arrived for his evening class. Each lesson had deepened his understanding of Taekwondo and its rich historical and philosophical roots. He was eager to discover the story behind the next pattern and the lessons it would impart.

Master Lee called the class to order, his voice resonating with authority. "Tonight, we will study the sixth pattern: Joong Gun. This pattern is named after Ahn Joong-Gun, a Korean independence activist who is revered for his bravery and dedication to his country. His actions and ultimate sacrifice have left a profound legacy in Korea's fight for independence."

Sam's curiosity was piqued as Master Lee began to demonstrate the Joong Gun pattern. Each movement was powerful and decisive, reflecting the courage and determination of the historical figure it was named after. Sam followed along, trying to embody the strength and resolve that each motion required.

After class, Master Lee approached Sam with a thoughtful expression. "Sam, could you help me retrieve a framed picture from the storage room? It's an old photograph of Ahn Joong-Gun, and I'd like to share his story with you in more detail."

Sam nodded eagerly and made his way to the storage room, a small space filled with boxes and old memorabilia. As he searched for the photograph, his eyes fell upon the ancient belt once more, neatly folded on a high shelf. He reached for it, feeling the now-familiar surge of anticipation.

The moment his fingers touched the belt, the world around him dissolved into a swirl of colours. When the spinning stopped, Sam found himself standing in a bustling early 20th-century Korean street. The air was filled with the sounds of street vendors, carriages, and the chatter of people going about their daily lives.

"Welcome, Sam," the old man's voice greeted him. Turning, Sam saw his wise guide standing beside him, a solemn expression on his face.

"Where are we now?" Sam asked, taking in the unfamiliar surroundings.

"This is Korea during the Japanese occupation," the old man explained. "You are here to learn about Ahn Joong-Gun, a patriot and freedom fighter who made the ultimate sacrifice for his country. His story is one of courage, determination, and unwavering dedication to the cause of Korean independence."

As the old man spoke, the scene shifted, and Sam found himself in a small, dimly lit room. A group of men sat around a table, deep in discussion. At the head of the table sat a young man with intense eyes and a resolute expression—Ahn Joong-Gun.

"Ahn Joong-Gun was deeply committed to freeing Korea from Japanese rule," the old man continued. "He believed that Korea deserved to be an independent and sovereign nation. His most famous act was the assassination of Ito Hirobumi, the former Resident-General of Korea, in Harbin, China, in 1909. This was a bold and risky move aimed at drawing international attention to Korea's plight."

The scene changed again, and Sam saw Ahn Joong-Gun standing in a courtroom, facing his accusers with calm defiance. Despite the gravity of his situation, there was a sense of peace and resolve in his demeanour.

"Ahn Joong-Gun was arrested and tried by the Japanese authorities," the old man said. "He was sentenced to death, but he faced his fate with dignity and unwavering belief in his cause.

Before his execution, he wrote several letters and essays, expressing his hopes for Korea's future and the importance of unity and education."

As Sam absorbed these lessons, he felt a deep respect for Ahn Joong-Gun's legacy. He realized that the pattern Joong Gun in Taekwondo was more than a series of movements; it was a tribute to a man who gave his life for his country's independence, embodying the principles of courage, sacrifice, and patriotism.

The old man placed a hand on Sam's shoulder. "Remember, Sam, the true strength of Taekwondo lies not only in physical prowess but in the courage to stand up for what is right, the willingness to sacrifice for the greater good, and the dedication to a cause greater than oneself. Ahn Joong-Gun's story teaches us the importance of bravery, selflessness, and patriotism."

The world around Sam began to blur once more, and he felt the familiar pull back to the present. When he opened his eyes, he was back in the storage room, the ancient belt still in his hand.

Master Lee's voice called out from the doorway. "Did you find the photograph, Sam?"

Quickly, Sam located the framed picture of Ahn Joong-Gun and handed it to Master Lee. "Thank you, Sam. You seem to be gaining a deeper understanding of the patterns with each lesson."

As Sam left the dojang, he felt a profound sense of inspiration. He understood now that each Taekwondo pattern was not only a physical exercise but a journey into the depths of history and philosophy. With every lesson, he was not only learning the art of Taekwondo but also the courage and dedication that came with it.

Walking home, Sam felt a renewed sense of purpose. He was eager to continue his journey, to learn more about the legends and teachings behind each pattern, and to embody the values they represented in his own life. The story of Ahn Joong-Gun had taught him that true strength and heroism came from the willingness to stand up for what is right and the dedication to a cause greater than oneself. These lessons would guide him both in and out of the dojang, shaping his path as a martial artist and a person.

Chapter 7: The Philosophy of Toi Gye

Toi Gye is the pen name of the noted scholar Yi Hwang (16th century), an authority on neo-Confucianism. The 37 movements of the pattern refer to his birthplace on 37 degrees latitude, the diagram represents "scholar".

37 Movements

The air was cool and crisp as Sam arrived at the dojang for his next Taekwondo class. Each lesson had been a voyage into the rich tapestry of Korean history, instilling in him a deep respect for the legends and heroes who had shaped the nation. He was eager to discover the story behind the next pattern and the wisdom it would impart.

Master Lee gathered the students together, his presence calm and authoritative. "Tonight, we will explore the seventh pattern: Toi Gye. This pattern is named after Yi Hwang, one of Korea's most esteemed Confucian scholars, who is also known by his pen name, Toi Gye. His contributions to Korean Confucianism and education are profound and enduring."

Sam watched attentively as Master Lee demonstrated the Toi Gye pattern. Each movement was deliberate and graceful, reflecting the deep intellectual and philosophical underpinnings of Yi Hwang's teachings. Sam followed along, striving to capture the essence of the scholar's wisdom in his motions.

After class, Master Lee approached Sam with a thoughtful expression. "Sam, could you help me retrieve a book from the library? It's a collection of Yi Hwang's writings, stored in the back."

Sam nodded eagerly and made his way to the library, a quiet room filled with rows of ancient books and manuscripts. As he searched through the shelves, his eyes fell upon the ancient belt, neatly folded on a high shelf. He reached for it, feeling the familiar surge of anticipation.

The moment his fingers touched the belt, the world around him dissolved into a swirl of colours. When the spinning stopped, Sam found himself standing in a serene garden, surrounded by scholars dressed in traditional Korean hanbok. The air was filled with the scent of blooming flowers and the soft rustle of leaves.

"Welcome, Sam," the old man's voice greeted him. Turning, Sam saw his wise guide standing beside him, a gentle smile on his face.

"Where are we now?" Sam asked, taking in the peaceful surroundings.

"This is Dosan Seowon, an academy established by Yi Hwang during the Joseon Dynasty," the old man explained. "You are here to learn about Yi Hwang, also known as Toi Gye, a revered Confucian scholar whose teachings have had a lasting impact on Korean philosophy and education."

As the old man spoke, the scene shifted, and Sam found himself in a modest study. A distinguished scholar sat at a desk, diligently writing by the light of an oil lamp. Sam recognized him from the descriptions he had read—this was Yi Hwang, deep in thought and surrounded by books and scrolls.

"Yi Hwang was a brilliant thinker and educator," the old man continued. "He wrote extensively on Confucian philosophy, emphasizing the importance of self-cultivation, moral integrity, and the harmonious relationship between humanity and nature. His works, such as 'The Ten Diagrams on Sage Learning,' provide a comprehensive guide to living a virtuous and balanced life."

The scene changed again, and Sam saw Yi Hwang teaching a group of students in a courtyard. His voice was calm and authoritative as he explained the principles of Confucianism, emphasizing the importance of righteousness, filial piety, and the pursuit of knowledge.

"Toi Gye's teachings were grounded in the belief that true wisdom comes from self-reflection and continuous learning," the old man said. "He believed that individuals should strive to cultivate their moral character and seek harmony within themselves and with the world around them."

As Sam absorbed these lessons, he felt a deep respect for Yi Hwang's legacy. He realized that the pattern Toi Gye in Taekwondo was more than a series of movements; it was a tribute to a man who dedicated his life to the pursuit of knowledge and the betterment of society through education and philosophy.

The old man placed a hand on Sam's shoulder. "Remember, Sam, the true strength of Taekwondo lies not only in physical prowess but in the wisdom and integrity you cultivate within yourself. Toi Gye's story teaches us the importance of continuous learning, self-cultivation, and the pursuit of harmony and balance."

The world around Sam began to blur once more, and he felt the familiar pull back to the present. When he opened his eyes, he was back in the library, the ancient belt still in his hand.

Master Lee's voice called out from the doorway. "Did you find the book, Sam?"

Quickly, Sam located the collection of Yi Hwang's writings and handed it to Master Lee. "Thank you, Sam. You seem to be gaining a deeper understanding of the patterns with each lesson."

As Sam left the dojang, he felt a profound sense of intellectual fulfilment. He understood now that each Taekwondo pattern was not only a physical exercise but a journey into the depths of history and philosophy. With every lesson, he was not only learning the art of Taekwondo but also the wisdom and enlightenment that came with it.

Walking home, Sam felt a renewed sense of purpose. He was eager to continue his journey, to learn more about the legends and teachings behind each pattern, and to embody the values they represented in his own life. The story of Yi Hwang, or Toi Gye, had taught him that true strength and enlightenment came from the pursuit of knowledge, self-cultivation, and the harmonious balance between oneself and the world. These lessons would guide him both in and out of the dojang, shaping his path as a martial artist and a person.

Chapter 8: The Legacy of Hwa Rang

Hwa Rang is named after the Hwa-Rang youth group which originated in the Silla Dynasty in the early 7th century. The 29 movements refer to the 29th Infantry Division, where Taekwon-Do developed into maturity.

29 Movements

The sky was painted with hues of orange and pink as Sam made his way to the dojang for his evening class. Each lesson had been a profound journey into the rich history and philosophy of Taekwondo, instilling in him a deep respect for the values and heroes that shaped the art. He was eager to discover the story behind the next pattern and the lessons it would impart.

Master Lee called the class to order, his voice calm and authoritative. "Tonight, we will study the eighth pattern: Hwa Rang. This pattern is named after the Hwa Rang, an elite group of young warriors from the Silla Dynasty. The Hwa Rang played a significant role in unifying the Korean peninsula and are remembered for their courage, loyalty, and code of honour."

Sam watched intently as Master Lee demonstrated the Hwa Rang pattern. Each movement was powerful and precise, reflecting the discipline and valour of the ancient warriors. Sam followed along, striving to embody the spirit and strength that each motion required.

After class, Master Lee approached Sam with a thoughtful expression. "Sam, could you help me retrieve a scroll from the library? It's an ancient text about the Hwa Rang, stored in the back."

Sam nodded eagerly and made his way to the library, a quiet room filled with rows of ancient books and manuscripts. As he searched through the shelves, his eyes fell upon the ancient belt, neatly folded on a high shelf. He reached for it, feeling the familiar surge of anticipation.

The moment his fingers touched the belt, the world around him dissolved into a swirl of colours. When the spinning stopped, Sam found himself standing in a lush forest, surrounded by a group of young warriors dressed in traditional Korean attire. The air was filled with the sound of rustling leaves and the distant call of a trumpet.

"Welcome, Sam," the old man's voice greeted him. Turning, Sam saw his wise guide standing beside him, a serene smile on his face.

"Where are we now?" Sam asked, taking in the vibrant surroundings.

"This is the Silla Dynasty, in the training grounds of the Hwa Rang," the old man explained. "You are here to learn about the

Hwa Rang, an elite group of young warriors who played a crucial role in the unification of Korea. Their code of honour and dedication to their country are legendary."

As the old man spoke, the scene shifted, and Sam found himself in a spacious hall. A group of young men stood in formation, their expressions resolute and their bodies poised for action. At the front of the group stood a commanding figure, their leader, who began to speak with a voice that resonated with authority and passion.

"The Hwa Rang were more than just warriors," the old man continued. "They were scholars, poets, and leaders dedicated to the principles of loyalty, courage, and honour. They followed a strict code known as the 'Hwa Rang Do,' which emphasized virtues such as loyalty to the king, filial piety, trust among friends, courage in battle, and justice for all."

The scene changed again, and Sam saw the Hwa Rang in action, leading their troops into battle with fearless determination. Their skills in martial arts, strategy, and leadership were evident as they fought to protect their homeland and unify the Korean peninsula.

"The Hwa Rang were instrumental in the unification of the Three Kingdoms of Korea," the old man said. "Their dedication and valour inspired generations of warriors and leaders. Their legacy lives on in the principles of Taekwondo and the Hwa Rang pattern, which honours their spirit and commitment to excellence."

As Sam absorbed these lessons, he felt a deep respect for the Hwa Rang's legacy. He realized that the pattern Hwa Rang in Taekwondo was more than a series of movements; it was a tribute to a group of young warriors who embodied the highest ideals of courage, loyalty, and honour.

The old man placed a hand on Sam's shoulder. "Remember, Sam, the true strength of Taekwondo lies not only in physical prowess but in the virtues of loyalty, courage, and honour. The Hwa Rang's story teaches us the importance of these principles in our lives and in our practice of Taekwondo."

The world around Sam began to blur once more, and he felt the familiar pull back to the present. When he opened his eyes, he was back in the library, the ancient belt still in his hand.

Master Lee's voice called out from the doorway. "Did you find the scroll, Sam?"

Quickly, Sam located the ancient scroll about the Hwa Rang and handed it to Master Lee. "Thank you, Sam. You seem to be gaining a deeper understanding of the patterns with each lesson."

As Sam left the dojang, he felt a profound sense of inspiration. He understood now that each Taekwondo pattern was not only a physical exercise but a journey into the depths of history and philosophy. With every lesson, he was not only learning the art of Taekwondo but also the values and principles that came with it.

Walking home, Sam felt a renewed sense of purpose. He was eager to continue his journey, to learn more about the legends and teachings behind each pattern, and to embody the values they represented in his own life. The story of the Hwa Rang had taught him that true strength and heroism came from the virtues of loyalty, courage, and honour. These lessons would guide him both in and out of the dojang, shaping his path as a martial artist and a person.

Chapter 9: The Legacy of Choong Moo

Choong Moo was the name given to the great Admiral Yi Soon-Sin of the Lee Dynasty. He was reputed to have invented the first armoured battleship (Kobukson) in 1592, which is said to be the precursor of the present day submarine. The reason why this pattern ends with a left hand attack is to symbolize his regrettable death, having no chance to show his unrestrained potentiality checked by the forced reservation of his loyalty to the king.

30 Movements

The evening sky was a deep, tranquil blue as Sam approached the dojang for his next Taekwondo lesson. His journey through the history and philosophy embedded in each Taekwondo pattern had been enlightening, filling him with respect and admiration for the legends and heroes who shaped Korean heritage. He was eager to discover the story behind the next pattern and the values it held.

Master Lee gathered the students together, his voice calm and resonant with authority. "Tonight, we will study the ninth pattern: Choong Moo. This pattern is named after Admiral Yi Sun-sin, who is also known by his posthumous title, Choong

Moo. Admiral Yi was one of Korea's greatest naval commanders, renowned for his strategic brilliance and unwavering loyalty."

Sam watched intently as Master Lee demonstrated the Choong Moo pattern. Each movement was precise and powerful, reflecting the strategic mind and indomitable spirit of the great admiral. Sam followed along, striving to embody the strength and resolve that each motion required.

After class, Master Lee approached Sam with a thoughtful expression. "Sam, could you help me retrieve a historical text from the library? It's a biography of Admiral Yi Sun-sin, stored in the back."

Sam nodded eagerly and made his way to the library, a quiet room filled with rows of ancient books and manuscripts. As he searched through the shelves, his eyes fell upon the ancient belt, neatly folded on a high shelf. He reached for it, feeling the familiar surge of anticipation.

The moment his fingers touched the belt, the world around him dissolved into a swirl of colours. When the spinning stopped, Sam found himself standing on the deck of a grand naval ship, surrounded by the sounds of the sea and the distant cries of seagulls. The ship was bustling with activity, sailors moving swiftly and efficiently under the command of a formidable figure.

"Welcome, Sam," the old man's voice greeted him. Turning, Sam saw his wise guide standing beside him, a serene smile on his face.

"Where are we now?" Sam asked, taking in the vibrant surroundings.

"This is the flagship of Admiral Yi Sun-sin during the Joseon Dynasty," the old man explained. "You are here to learn about Admiral Yi, a naval commander whose strategic genius and unyielding loyalty saved Korea from invasion on multiple occasions. His legacy is a testament to the virtues of courage, wisdom, and devotion to one's country."

As the old man spoke, the scene shifted, and Sam found himself in the midst of a naval battle. Admiral Yi stood at the helm, his presence commanding and calm despite the chaos around him. His strategic mind was evident as he directed his fleet with precision, outmanoeuvring the enemy with remarkable skill.

"Admiral Yi Sun-sin is best known for his victories during the Imjin War, where he employed innovative tactics and superior naval strategies to defeat a much larger Japanese fleet," the old man continued. "His most famous battle was the Battle of Myeongnyang, where he led just 13 ships against an invading fleet of 133 Japanese warships, emerging victorious against overwhelming odds."

The scene changed again, and Sam saw Admiral Yi in a quiet moment, writing in his war diary. His entries reflected not only his strategic insights but also his deep sense of duty and responsibility. Despite numerous challenges and betrayals, Admiral Yi remained steadfast in his commitment to his country and his people.

"Admiral Yi's dedication and unwavering loyalty were matched by his humility and integrity," the old man said. "He once said, 'Those willing to die will live, and those willing to live will die.' This mindset, combined with his strategic brilliance, made him an extraordinary leader and a revered hero in Korean history."

As Sam absorbed these lessons, he felt a deep respect for Admiral Yi Sun-sin's legacy. He realized that the pattern Choong Moo in Taekwondo was more than a series of movements; it was a tribute to a man who exemplified courage, wisdom, and unwavering loyalty in the face of great adversity.

The old man placed a hand on Sam's shoulder. "Remember, Sam, the true strength of Taekwondo lies not only in physical prowess but in the virtues of courage, wisdom, and loyalty. Admiral Yi's story teaches us the importance of these principles in our lives and in our practice of Taekwondo."

The world around Sam began to blur once more, and he felt the familiar pull back to the present. When he opened his eyes, he was back in the library, the ancient belt still in his hand.

Master Lee's voice called out from the doorway. "Did you find the text, Sam?"

Quickly, Sam located the biography of Admiral Yi Sun-sin and handed it to Master Lee. "Thank you, Sam. You seem to be gaining a deeper understanding of the patterns with each lesson."

As Sam left the dojang, he felt a profound sense of inspiration. He understood now that each Taekwondo pattern was not only a physical exercise but a journey into the depths of history and philosophy. With every lesson, he was not only learning the art of Taekwondo but also the values and principles that came with it.

Walking home, Sam felt a renewed sense of purpose. He was eager to continue his journey, to learn more about the legends and teachings behind each pattern, and to embody the values they represented in his own life. The story of Admiral Yi Sun-sin had taught him that true strength and heroism came from the virtues of courage, wisdom, and unwavering loyalty. These lessons would guide him both in and out of the dojang, shaping his path as a martial artist and a person.

Chapter 10: The Conquests of Kwang Gae

Kwang Gae is named after the famous Kwang-Gae-Toh-Wang, the 19th King of the Koguryo Dynasty, who regained all the lost territories including the greater part of Manchuria. The diagram (+) represents the expansion and recovery of lost territory. The 39 movements refer to the first two figures of 391 A.D., the year he came to the throne.

39 Movements

The dojang was quiet as Sam arrived for his next lesson, the stillness of the evening air amplifying his anticipation. Each Taekwondo pattern had revealed a rich tapestry of history and philosophy, and he was eager to uncover the story behind the next pattern and the values it would impart.

Master Lee called the class to order, his voice steady and authoritative. "Tonight, we will study the tenth pattern: Kwang Gae. This pattern is named after Gwanggaeto the Great, the 19th ruler of the Goguryeo dynasty. He was a king renowned for his military conquests and for expanding the territory of Korea to its greatest extent."

Sam watched intently as Master Lee demonstrated the Kwang Gae pattern. Each movement was powerful and expansive, reflecting the king's ambition and strategic brilliance. Sam followed along, striving to capture the strength and vision that each motion required.

After class, Master Lee approached Sam with a thoughtful expression. "Sam, could you help me retrieve a map from the library? It's an old map depicting the territories conquered by Gwanggaeto the Great."

Sam nodded eagerly and made his way to the library, a quiet room filled with rows of ancient books and scrolls. As he searched through the shelves, his eyes fell upon the ancient belt, neatly folded on a high shelf. He reached for it, feeling the familiar surge of anticipation.

The moment his fingers touched the belt, the world around him dissolved into a swirl of colours. When the spinning stopped, Sam found himself standing on a vast battlefield, surrounded by soldiers clad in traditional armour. The air was filled with the sounds of clashing swords and the shouts of warriors.

"Welcome, Sam," the old man's voice greeted him. Turning, Sam saw his wise guide standing beside him, a serene smile on his face.

"Where are we now?" Sam asked, taking in the vibrant surroundings.

"This is the battlefield of Gwanggaeto the Great during the Goguryeo dynasty," the old man explained. "You are here to learn about Gwanggaeto, a king whose military conquests and strategic brilliance expanded the territory of Korea to its greatest extent. His legacy is a testament to the virtues of vision, leadership, and determination."

As the old man spoke, the scene shifted, and Sam found himself in a grand hall. A tall, imposing figure sat on a throne, surrounded by advisors and generals. Sam recognized him as Gwanggaeto the Great, a ruler with a commanding presence and a keen mind.

"Gwanggaeto the Great was a visionary leader," the old man continued. "He ascended the throne at a young age and immediately set about expanding his kingdom. Under his rule, Goguryeo conquered vast territories, including parts of modern-day China, Russia, and Mongolia. His conquests not only expanded the kingdom but also brought stability and prosperity to his people."

The scene changed again, and Sam saw Gwanggaeto leading his troops into battle. His strategic brilliance was evident as he outmanoeuvred his enemies with tactical precision. Despite the chaos of war, there was a sense of order and purpose in his actions, reflecting his deep commitment to his people and his vision for a unified Korea.

"Gwanggaeto's achievements were not just military," the old man said. "He also worked to strengthen his kingdom internally, promoting trade, culture, and the arts. He understood that true power came not only from military might but also from the prosperity and well-being of his people."

As Sam absorbed these lessons, he felt a deep respect for Gwanggaeto's legacy. He realized that the pattern Kwang Gae in Taekwondo was more than a series of movements; it was a tribute to a king who embodied the ideals of vision, leadership, and determination.

The old man placed a hand on Sam's shoulder. "Remember, Sam, the true strength of Taekwondo lies not only in physical prowess but in the vision and leadership you cultivate within yourself. Gwanggaeto's story teaches us the importance of these principles in our lives and in our practice of Taekwondo."

The world around Sam began to blur once more, and he felt the familiar pull back to the present. When he opened his eyes, he was back in the library, the ancient belt still in his hand.

Master Lee's voice called out from the doorway. "Did you find the map, Sam?"

Quickly, Sam located the old map depicting Gwanggaeto's conquests and handed it to Master Lee. "Thank you, Sam. You seem to be gaining a deeper understanding of the patterns with each lesson."

As Sam left the dojang, he felt a profound sense of inspiration. He understood now that each Taekwondo pattern was not only a physical exercise but a journey into the depths of history and philosophy. With every lesson, he was not only learning the art of Taekwondo but also the values and principles that came with it.

Walking home, Sam felt a renewed sense of purpose. He was eager to continue his journey, to learn more about the legends and teachings behind each pattern, and to embody the values they represented in his own life. The story of Gwanggaeto the Great had taught him that true strength and heroism came from the virtues of vision, leadership, and determination. These lessons would guide him both in and out of the dojang, shaping his path as a martial artist and a person.

Chapter 11: The Integrity of Po Eun

Po Eun is the pseudonym of a loyal subject Chong Mong-Chu (1400) who was a famous poet and whose poem "I would not serve a second master though I might be crucified a hundred times" is known to every Korean. He was also a pioneer in the field of physics. The diagram (-) represents his unerring loyalty to the king and country towards the end of the Koryo Dynasty.

36 Movements

The sun was beginning to set, casting a warm glow over the dojang as Sam arrived for his next Taekwondo lesson. Each class had been an enlightening journey into the heart of Korean history and philosophy, and he was eager to uncover the story behind the next pattern.

Master Lee called the class to order, his voice calm and authoritative. "Tonight, we will study the eleventh pattern: Po Eun. This pattern is named after Jeong Mong-ju, also known by his pen name Po Eun, a revered scholar and statesman of the Goryeo Dynasty. He is remembered for his unwavering loyalty and integrity."

Sam watched attentively as Master Lee demonstrated the Po Eun pattern. Each movement was deliberate and dignified, reflecting the steadfastness and moral strength of Jeong Mong-ju. Sam followed along, striving to capture the essence of integrity and honour that each motion required.

After class, Master Lee approached Sam with a thoughtful expression. "Sam, could you help me retrieve a book from the library? It's a collection of Jeong Mong-ju's poetry, stored in the back."

Sam nodded eagerly and made his way to the library, a quiet room filled with rows of ancient books and manuscripts. As he searched through the shelves, his eyes fell upon the ancient belt, neatly folded on a high shelf. He reached for it, feeling the familiar surge of anticipation.

The moment his fingers touched the belt, the world around him dissolved into a swirl of colours. When the spinning stopped, Sam found himself standing in a serene garden, surrounded by the sounds of flowing water and the chirping of birds. The garden was meticulously maintained, reflecting a sense of order and harmony.

"Welcome, Sam," the old man's voice greeted him. Turning, Sam saw his wise guide standing beside him, a gentle smile on his face.

"Where are we now?" Sam asked, taking in the tranquil surroundings.

"This is the residence of Jeong Mong-ju during the Goryeo Dynasty," the old man explained. "You are here to learn about Po Eun, a scholar and statesman whose unwavering loyalty and integrity have made him a symbol of fidelity and righteousness in Korean history."

As the old man spoke, the scene shifted, and Sam found himself in a grand hall. A dignified figure stood before a group of scholars, his presence calm and commanding. Sam recognized him as Jeong Mong-ju, a man of great wisdom and moral strength.

"Jeong Mong-ju was not only a brilliant scholar but also a dedicated statesman," the old man continued. "He served as an advisor to the king and was deeply respected for his integrity and unwavering loyalty to the Goryeo Dynasty, even during times of political turmoil and transition."

The scene changed again, and Sam saw Jeong Mong-ju in a moment of profound decision. He was approached by emissaries from the emerging Joseon Dynasty, who tried to persuade him to switch allegiances. Despite the pressures and temptations, Jeong Mong-ju remained steadfast in his loyalty to the Goryeo Dynasty, a decision that would ultimately cost him his life.

"Jeong Mong-ju's loyalty was tested in the most severe way," the old man said. "Even in the face of death, he chose to remain true to his principles and his commitment to the Goryeo Dynasty. His final poem, written on the eve of his assassination, is a poignant testament to his integrity and unwavering resolve."

As Sam absorbed these lessons, he felt a deep respect for Jeong Mong-ju's legacy. He realized that the pattern Po Eun in Taekwondo was more than a series of movements; it was a tribute to a man who embodied the highest ideals of loyalty, integrity, and honour.

The old man placed a hand on Sam's shoulder. "Remember, Sam, the true strength of Taekwondo lies not only in physical prowess but in the integrity and moral strength you cultivate within yourself. Po Eun's story teaches us the importance of remaining true to our principles and values, even in the face of great adversity."

The world around Sam began to blur once more, and he felt the familiar pull back to the present. When he opened his eyes, he was back in the library, the ancient belt still in his hand.

Master Lee's voice called out from the doorway. "Did you find the book, Sam?"

Quickly, Sam located the collection of Jeong Mong-ju's poetry and handed it to Master Lee. "Thank you, Sam. You seem to be gaining a deeper understanding of the patterns with each lesson."

As Sam left the dojang, he felt a profound sense of inspiration. He understood now that each Taekwondo pattern was not only a physical exercise but a journey into the depths of history and philosophy. With every lesson, he was not only learning the art of Taekwondo but also the values and principles that came with it.

Walking home, Sam felt a renewed sense of purpose. He was eager to continue his journey, to learn more about the legends and teachings behind each pattern, and to embody the values they represented in his own life. The story of Jeong Mong-ju had taught him that true strength and heroism came from the virtues of loyalty, integrity, and unwavering commitment to one's principles. These lessons would guide him both in and out of the dojang, shaping his path as a martial artist and a person.

Chapter 12: The Valour of Ge Baek

Ge Baek is named after Ge-Baek, a great general in the Baek Je Dynasty (660 A.D.). The diagram (|) represents his severe and strict military discipline.

44 Movements

The dojang was bathed in the soft light of early evening as Sam arrived for his next Taekwondo lesson. The air buzzed with the energy of his classmates, each eager to delve into the story behind the next pattern. Each pattern had offered Sam a profound insight into Korean history and values, and he was excited to discover what new lessons awaited him.

Master Lee called the class to order, his voice calm and authoritative. "Tonight, we will study the twelfth pattern: Ge Baek. This pattern is named after General Ge Baek, a renowned military commander of the Baekje Dynasty. He is remembered for his unwavering courage and leadership in the face of overwhelming odds."

Sam watched intently as Master Lee demonstrated the Ge Baek pattern. Each movement was forceful and decisive, reflecting the indomitable spirit and tactical brilliance of General Ge Baek. Sam followed along, striving to embody the strength and determination that each motion required.

After class, Master Lee approached Sam with a thoughtful expression. "Sam, could you help me retrieve a historical account from the library? It's an old text about the final stand of General Ge Baek, stored in the back."

Sam nodded eagerly and made his way to the library, a quiet room filled with rows of ancient books and scrolls. As he searched through the shelves, his eyes fell upon the ancient belt, neatly folded on a high shelf. He reached for it, feeling the familiar surge of anticipation.

The moment his fingers touched the belt, the world around him dissolved into a swirl of colours. When the spinning stopped, Sam found himself standing on a vast battlefield, surrounded by soldiers clad in traditional armour. The air was thick with the sounds of clashing swords and the shouts of warriors.

"Welcome, Sam," the old man's voice greeted him. Turning, Sam saw his wise guide standing beside him, a serene smile on his face.

"Where are we now?" Sam asked, taking in the intense surroundings.

"This is the battlefield of Hwangsanbeol during the Baekje Dynasty," the old man explained. "You are here to learn about General Ge Baek, a military leader known for his courage and strategic brilliance. Despite facing overwhelming odds, he led his troops with unwavering resolve and is remembered as a symbol of bravery and loyalty."

As the old man spoke, the scene shifted, and Sam found himself in a grand military camp. A tall, imposing figure stood at the centre, surrounded by his officers. Sam recognized him as General Ge Baek, a man whose presence commanded respect and loyalty from his troops.

"General Ge Baek was faced with the daunting task of defending Baekje against the forces of Silla," the old man continued. "Despite being vastly outnumbered, he refused to retreat, choosing instead to make a stand for his homeland. His tactical brilliance and leadership inspired his soldiers to fight with extraordinary valour."

The scene changed again, and Sam saw Ge Baek leading his troops into battle. His strategic mind was evident as he directed his forces with precision and determination. Despite the overwhelming enemy forces, Ge Baek's leadership and courage never wavered.

"Ge Baek's final stand at the Battle of Hwangsanbeol is a testament to his unyielding spirit," the old man said. "Knowing that defeat was inevitable, he chose to fight to the end, demonstrating the highest principles of loyalty and bravery. His sacrifice became a symbol of patriotic dedication and has been remembered throughout Korean history."

As Sam absorbed these lessons, he felt a deep respect for General Ge Baek's legacy. He realized that the pattern Ge Baek in Taekwondo was more than a series of movements; it was a tribute to a man who embodied the ideals of courage, leadership, and unwavering loyalty to his country.

The old man placed a hand on Sam's shoulder. "Remember, Sam, the true strength of Taekwondo lies not only in physical prowess but in the courage and leadership you cultivate within yourself. Ge Baek's story teaches us the importance of standing firm in our principles and leading with integrity, even in the face of overwhelming odds."

The world around Sam began to blur once more, and he felt the familiar pull back to the present. When he opened his eyes, he was back in the library, the ancient belt still in his hand.

Master Lee's voice called out from the doorway. "Did you find the text, Sam?"

Quickly, Sam located the historical account of General Ge Baek and handed it to Master Lee. "Thank you, Sam. You seem to be gaining a deeper understanding of the patterns with each lesson."

As Sam left the dojang, he felt a profound sense of inspiration. He understood now that each Taekwondo pattern was not only a physical exercise but a journey into the depths of history and philosophy. With every lesson, he was not only learning the art of Taekwondo but also the values and principles that came with it.

Walking home, Sam felt a renewed sense of purpose. He was eager to continue his journey, to learn more about the legends and teachings behind each pattern, and to embody the values they represented in his own life. The story of General Ge Baek had taught him that true strength and heroism came from the virtues of courage, leadership, and unwavering dedication to one's principles. These lessons would guide him both in and out of the dojang, shaping his path as a martial artist and a person.

Chapter 13: The Vision of Eui Am

Eui Am is the pseudonym of Son Byong Hi, leader of the Korean independence movement on March 1, 1919. The 45 movements refer to his age when he changed the name of Dong Hak (Oriental Culture) to Chondo Kyo (Heavenly Way Religion) in 1905. The diagram (|) represents his indomitable spirit, displayed while dedicating himself to the prosperity of his nation.

45 Movements

The dojang was filled with the low hum of conversation as Sam entered for his next Taekwondo lesson. Each class had brought him closer to understanding the rich tapestry of Korean history and the values that underpin Taekwondo. He was eager to delve into the story behind the next pattern and the wisdom it held.

Master Lee called the class to order, his voice calm and commanding. "Tonight, we will study the thirteenth pattern: Eui Am. This pattern is named after Son Byong-hi, also known as Eui Am, a prominent leader in the Korean independence movement and the founder of the Cheondogyo religion. He is remembered for his vision, resilience, and dedication to his people's spiritual and national liberation."

Sam watched attentively as Master Lee demonstrated the Eui Am pattern. Each movement was deliberate and purposeful, reflecting the profound spiritual strength and unwavering commitment of Son Byong-hi. Sam followed along, striving to embody the vision and resilience that each motion required.

After class, Master Lee approached Sam with a thoughtful expression. "Sam, could you help me retrieve a document from the library? It's a manifesto written by Son Byong-hi, stored in the back."

Sam nodded eagerly and made his way to the library, a quiet room filled with rows of ancient books and manuscripts. As he searched through the shelves, his eyes fell upon the ancient belt, neatly folded on a high shelf. He reached for it, feeling the familiar surge of anticipation.

The moment his fingers touched the belt, the world around him dissolved into a swirl of colours. When the spinning stopped, Sam found himself standing in a bustling city, surrounded by people in traditional Korean attire. The air was filled with a sense of urgency and determination.

"Welcome, Sam," the old man's voice greeted him. Turning, Sam saw his wise guide standing beside him, a gentle smile on his face.

"Where are we now?" Sam asked, taking in the vibrant surroundings.

"This is Seoul during the late Joseon Dynasty," the old man explained. "You are here to learn about Son Byong-hi, a visionary leader who played a crucial role in Korea's struggle for independence and spiritual renewal. He founded the Cheondogyo religion, which emphasized human dignity and social reform."

As the old man spoke, the scene shifted, and Sam found himself in a large hall filled with passionate individuals. At the centre stood Son Byong-hi, a man of great spiritual presence and resolve, addressing the crowd with fervour and conviction.

"Son Byong-hi's vision extended beyond spiritual renewal," the old man continued. "He was deeply involved in the Korean independence movement, advocating for national sovereignty and human rights. His leadership in the March 1st Movement of 1919 was a pivotal moment in Korea's struggle for independence from Japanese rule."

The scene changed again, and Sam saw Son Byong-hi leading a peaceful demonstration. Despite the risks, his followers marched with unwavering determination, inspired by his vision of a free and just society. The peaceful protest was met with brutal repression, but the spirit of resistance and hope remained unbroken.

"Son Byong-hi's commitment to his people's freedom and dignity was unwavering," the old man said. "He believed that true liberation could only be achieved through the unity of spiritual and national renewal. His teachings emphasized the importance of moral integrity, social justice, and the intrinsic worth of every individual."

As Sam absorbed these lessons, he felt a deep respect for Son Byong-hi's legacy. He realized that the pattern Eui Am in Taekwondo was more than a series of movements; it was a tribute to a man who embodied the ideals of vision, resilience, and unwavering dedication to his people's spiritual and national liberation.

The old man placed a hand on Sam's shoulder. "Remember, Sam, the true strength of Taekwondo lies not only in physical prowess but in the vision and resilience you cultivate within yourself. Eui Am's story teaches us the importance of striving for a just and free society, grounded in moral integrity and human dignity."

The world around Sam began to blur once more, and he felt the familiar pull back to the present. When he opened his eyes, he was back in the library, the ancient belt still in his hand.

Master Lee's voice called out from the doorway. "Did you find the document, Sam?"

Quickly, Sam located the manifesto written by Son Byong-hi and handed it to Master Lee. "Thank you, Sam. You seem to be gaining a deeper understanding of the patterns with each lesson."

As Sam left the dojang, he felt a profound sense of inspiration. He understood now that each Taekwondo pattern was not only a physical exercise but a journey into the depths of history and philosophy. With every lesson, he was not only learning the art of Taekwondo but also the values and principles that came with it.

Walking home, Sam felt a renewed sense of purpose. He was eager to continue his journey, to learn more about the legends and teachings behind each pattern, and to embody the values they represented in his own life. The story of Son Byong-hi had taught him that true strength and heroism came from the virtues of vision, resilience, and unwavering dedication to the pursuit of justice and human dignity. These lessons would guide him both in and out of the dojang, shaping his path as a martial artist and a person.

Chapter 14: The Loyalty of Choong Jang

Choong Jang is the pseudonym given to General Kim Duk Ryang who lived during the Lee Dynasty, 14th century. This pattern ends with a left-hand attack to symbolize the tragedy of his death at 27 in prison before he was able to reach full maturity.

52 Movements

The dojang was quiet in the early morning light as Sam arrived for his next Taekwondo lesson. The stillness of the air filled him with a sense of anticipation, as each class had drawn him deeper into the rich history and values of Korea. Today, he was eager to uncover the story behind the next pattern and the lessons it held.

Master Lee called the class to order, his voice resonant with authority. "Today, we will study the fourteenth pattern: Choong Jang. This pattern is named after General Kim Duk Ryang, who held the title Choong Jang. He was a brilliant military leader during the Joseon Dynasty and is remembered for his unwavering loyalty and tragic heroism."

Sam watched attentively as Master Lee demonstrated the Choong Jang pattern. Each movement was swift and precise, reflecting the tactical genius and determined spirit of General Kim Duk Ryang. Sam followed along, striving to capture the loyalty and courage that each motion required.

After class, Master Lee approached Sam with a thoughtful expression. "Sam, could you help me retrieve a historical record from the library? It's an account of General Kim Duk Ryang's final battle, stored in the back."

Sam nodded eagerly and made his way to the library, a quiet room filled with rows of ancient books and manuscripts. As he searched through the shelves, his eyes fell upon the ancient belt, neatly folded on a high shelf. He reached for it, feeling the familiar surge of anticipation.

The moment his fingers touched the belt, the world around him dissolved into a swirl of colours. When the spinning stopped, Sam found himself standing on a rugged mountainside, surrounded by soldiers in traditional Korean armour. The air was charged with the tension of an impending battle.

"Welcome, Sam," the old man's voice greeted him. Turning, Sam saw his wise guide standing beside him, a gentle smile on his face.

"Where are we now?" Sam asked, taking in the intense surroundings.

"This is the site of General Kim Duk Ryang's final stand during the Joseon Dynasty," the old man explained. "You are here to learn about Choong Jang, a title that signifies unwavering loyalty and heroic sacrifice. General Kim Duk Ryang is remembered for his dedication to his country and his people, even in the face of certain death."

As the old man spoke, the scene shifted, and Sam found himself in a grand military camp. A tall, imposing figure stood at the centre, surrounded by his officers. Sam recognized him as General Kim Duk Ryang, a man whose presence commanded respect and loyalty from his troops.

"General Kim Duk Ryang was known for his tactical brilliance and his ability to inspire his soldiers," the old man continued. "He fought valiantly to defend the Joseon Dynasty against invading forces, often outnumbered and outmatched. His leadership and courage in battle became legendary."

The scene changed again, and Sam saw Kim Duk Ryang leading his troops into a fierce battle. Despite the overwhelming enemy forces, his strategic mind and indomitable spirit shone through. His soldiers fought with extraordinary bravery, inspired by their leader's unwavering resolve.

"Kim Duk Ryang's final stand was marked by tragic heroism," the old man said. "Knowing that defeat was inevitable, he chose to fight to the end, refusing to surrender. His sacrifice became a powerful symbol of loyalty and honour in Korean history."

As Sam absorbed these lessons, he felt a deep respect for Kim Duk Ryang's legacy. He realized that the pattern Choong Jang in Taekwondo was more than a series of movements; it was a tribute to a man who embodied the ideals of loyalty, courage, and self-sacrifice.

The old man placed a hand on Sam's shoulder. "Remember, Sam, the true strength of Taekwondo lies not only in physical prowess but in the loyalty and courage you cultivate within yourself. Choong Jang's story teaches us the importance of standing firm in our commitments and values, even in the face of overwhelming challenges."

The world around Sam began to blur once more, and he felt the familiar pull back to the present. When he opened his eyes, he was back in the library, the ancient belt still in his hand.

Master Lee's voice called out from the doorway. "Did you find the record, Sam?"

Quickly, Sam located the historical account of General Kim Duk Ryang's final battle and handed it to Master Lee. "Thank you, Sam. You seem to be gaining a deeper understanding of the patterns with each lesson."

As Sam left the dojang, he felt a profound sense of inspiration. He understood now that each Taekwondo pattern was not only a physical exercise but a journey into the depths of history and philosophy. With every lesson, he was not only learning the art of Taekwondo but also the values and principles that came with it.

Walking home, Sam felt a renewed sense of purpose. He was eager to continue his journey, to learn more about the legends and teachings behind each pattern, and to embody the values they represented in his own life. The story of General Kim Duk Ryang had taught him that true strength and heroism came from the virtues of loyalty, courage, and self-sacrifice. These lessons would guide him both in and out of the dojang, shaping his path as a martial artist and a person.

Chapter 15: The Philosophy of Juche

Juche is a philosophical idea that man is the master of everything and decides everything, in other words, the idea that man is the master of the world and his own destiny. It is said that this idea was rooted in Baekdu Mountain which symbolizes the spirit of the Korean people. The diagram (|) represents Baekdu Mountain.

45 Movements

The dojang was alive with the energy of focused practice as Sam arrived for his next Taekwondo lesson. Each class had been a journey through time, revealing the rich history and deep values of Korean culture. Today, Sam was eager to learn about the next pattern and the insights it held.

Master Lee called the class to order, his voice calm and resonant. "Today, we will study the fifteenth pattern: Juche. This pattern represents the philosophy of self-reliance and independence, a core principle that has shaped the Korean spirit and its historical journey."

Sam watched intently as Master Lee demonstrated the Juche pattern. Each movement was powerful and assertive, embodying the strength and confidence of self-reliance. Sam followed along, striving to internalize the philosophy of independence and determination that each motion required.

After class, Master Lee approached Sam with a thoughtful expression. "Sam, could you help me retrieve a text from the library? It's a philosophical treatise on Juche, stored in the back."

Sam nodded eagerly and made his way to the library, a quiet room filled with rows of ancient books and manuscripts. As he searched through the shelves, his eyes fell upon the ancient belt, neatly folded on a high shelf. He reached for it, feeling the familiar surge of anticipation.

The moment his fingers touched the belt, the world around him dissolved into a swirl of colours. When the spinning stopped, Sam found himself standing on a mountaintop, overlooking a vast and rugged landscape. The air was crisp and clear, filled with a sense of boundless possibility.

"Welcome, Sam," the old man's voice greeted him. Turning, Sam saw his wise guide standing beside him, a serene smile on his face.

"Where are we now?" Sam asked, taking in the expansive surroundings.

"This is the symbolic birthplace of the Juche philosophy," the old man explained. "You are here to learn about the principle of self-reliance and independence that has been a cornerstone of Korean resilience and progress. Juche teaches that humans are the masters of their own destiny, capable of shaping their future through their efforts and determination."

As the old man spoke, the scene shifted, and Sam found himself in a modest yet bustling village. The people around him worked diligently, each contributing to the well-being of the community. Their faces reflected a sense of purpose and self-assurance.

"The Juche philosophy emphasizes the importance of self-reliance and the collective effort of individuals to build a strong and independent society," the old man continued. "It encourages people to rely on their own abilities and resources, fostering a spirit of innovation and resilience."

The scene changed again, and Sam saw a group of leaders discussing plans for the development of their community. Their discussions were marked by a focus on self-sufficiency and the empowerment of the people. The determination to forge their own path, free from external control, was evident in their resolve.

"Juche is not just a political or economic philosophy; it is a way of life," the old man said. "It teaches us to believe in our own potential and to take responsibility for our own destiny. This principle has guided the Korean people through times of hardship and transformation, helping them to overcome challenges and achieve progress."

As Sam absorbed these lessons, he felt a deep respect for the philosophy of Juche. He realized that the pattern Juche in Taekwondo was more than a series of movements; it was a tribute to the enduring spirit of self-reliance and independence that had shaped Korean history and culture.

The old man placed a hand on Sam's shoulder. "Remember, Sam, the true strength of Taekwondo lies not only in physical prowess but in the self-reliance and determination you cultivate within yourself. Juche's philosophy teaches us the importance of believing in our own abilities and taking control of our own destiny."

The world around Sam began to blur once more, and he felt the familiar pull back to the present. When he opened his eyes, he was back in the library, the ancient belt still in his hand.

Master Lee's voice called out from the doorway. "Did you find the text, Sam?"

Quickly, Sam located the philosophical treatise on Juche and handed it to Master Lee. "Thank you, Sam. You seem to be gaining a deeper understanding of the patterns with each lesson."

As Sam left the dojang, he felt a profound sense of inspiration. He understood now that each Taekwondo pattern was not only a physical exercise but a journey into the depths of history and philosophy. With every lesson, he was not only learning the art of Taekwondo but also the values and principles that came with it.

Walking home, Sam felt a renewed sense of purpose. He was eager to continue his journey, to learn more about the legends and teachings behind each pattern, and to embody the values they represented in his own life. The philosophy of Juche had taught him that true strength and heroism came from the virtues of self-reliance, determination, and the unwavering belief in one's ability to shape their own destiny. These lessons would guide him both in and out of the dojang, shaping his path as a martial artist and a person.

Chapter 16: The Spirit of Sam Il

Sam Il denotes the historical date of the independence movement of Korea which began throughout the country on March 1, 1919. The 33 movements in the pattern stand for the 33 patriots who planned the movement.

33 Movements

The dojang was bathed in the warm glow of the afternoon sun as Sam arrived for his next Taekwondo lesson. Each class had taken him on a journey through history, revealing the profound values and traditions that shaped Korea. Today, Sam was eager to learn about the next pattern and the lessons it held.

Master Lee called the class to order, his voice calm and resonant. "Today, we will study the sixteenth pattern: Sam Il. This pattern commemorates March 1st, 1919, a significant date in Korean history when the Korean people rose in a nationwide demonstration for independence from Japanese rule. The spirit of Sam Il represents the enduring quest for freedom and the resilience of the human spirit."

Sam watched attentively as Master Lee demonstrated the Sam Il pattern. Each movement was forceful and resolute, embodying the determination and courage of the Korean independence movement. Sam followed along, striving to internalize the spirit of defiance and hope that each motion required.

After class, Master Lee approached Sam with a thoughtful expression. "Sam, could you help me retrieve a historical document from the library? It's a declaration from the March 1st Movement, stored in the back."

Sam nodded eagerly and made his way to the library, a quiet room filled with rows of ancient books and manuscripts. As he searched through the shelves, his eyes fell upon the ancient belt, neatly folded on a high shelf. He reached for it, feeling the familiar surge of anticipation.

The moment his fingers touched the belt, the world around him dissolved into a swirl of colours. When the spinning stopped, Sam found himself standing in a bustling square, surrounded by people waving flags and holding signs. The air was filled with chants of "Mansei!"—a cry for long life and freedom.

"Welcome, Sam," the old man's voice greeted him. Turning, Sam saw his wise guide standing beside him, a serene smile on his face.

"Where are we now?" Sam asked, taking in the vibrant surroundings.

"This is Seoul on March 1st, 1919," the old man explained. "You are here to learn about the Sam Il Movement, a pivotal moment in Korean history when the people united to demand independence from Japanese rule. The spirit of Sam Il represents the unwavering desire for freedom and the resilience of the Korean people."

As the old man spoke, the scene shifted, and Sam found himself in a crowded room filled with passionate individuals. At the centre stood a group of leaders, reading aloud the Declaration of Independence, their voices strong and firm.

"The March 1st Movement was a peaceful protest that spread throughout Korea," the old man continued. "It was inspired by the principle of self-determination and the desire for a free and independent nation. Despite the harsh repression by the Japanese authorities, the movement ignited a spirit of unity and resistance that would continue to inspire future generations."

The scene changed again, and Sam saw peaceful demonstrations turning into brutal confrontations as the Japanese military responded with force. Despite the violence, the Korean people's resolve did not falter. Their cries for independence echoed through the streets, a testament to their unbreakable spirit.

"The Sam Il Movement was marked by sacrifice and suffering," the old man said. "But it also showcased the resilience and courage of the Korean people. It was a declaration of their right to be free, and their determination to achieve that freedom, no matter the cost."

As Sam absorbed these lessons, he felt a deep respect for the legacy of the Sam Il Movement. He realized that the pattern Sam Il in Taekwondo was more than a series of movements; it was a tribute to the enduring quest for freedom and the resilience of the human spirit.

The old man placed a hand on Sam's shoulder. "Remember, Sam, the true strength of Taekwondo lies not only in physical prowess but in the resilience and determination you cultivate within yourself. The spirit of Sam Il teaches us the importance of standing up for our rights and persevering in the face of adversity."

The world around Sam began to blur once more, and he felt the familiar pull back to the present. When he opened his eyes, he was back in the library, the ancient belt still in his hand.

Master Lee's voice called out from the doorway. "Did you find the document, Sam?"

Quickly, Sam located the declaration from the March 1st Movement and handed it to Master Lee. "Thank you, Sam. You seem to be gaining a deeper understanding of the patterns with each lesson."

As Sam left the dojang, he felt a profound sense of inspiration. He understood now that each Taekwondo pattern was not only a physical exercise but a journey into the depths of history and philosophy. With every lesson, he was not only learning the art of Taekwondo but also the values and principles that came with it.

Walking home, Sam felt a renewed sense of purpose. He was eager to continue his journey, to learn more about the legends and teachings behind each pattern, and to embody the values they represented in his own life. The spirit of the Sam Il Movement had taught him that true strength and heroism came from the virtues of resilience, determination, and the unwavering quest for freedom. These lessons would guide him both in and out of the dojang, shaping his path as a martial artist and a person.

Chapter 17: The Bravery of Yoo Sin

Yoo Sin is named after General Kim Yoo Sin, a commanding general during the Silla Dynasty. The 68 movements refer to the last two figures of 668 A. D., the year Korea was united. The ready posture signifies a sword drawn on the right rather than left side, symbolizing Yoo Sin's mistake of following his king's orders to fight with foreign forces against his own nation.

68 Movements

The dojang was vibrant with the energy of eager students as Sam entered for his next Taekwondo lesson. Each class had deepened his understanding of Taekwondo's rich history and the values that shaped it. Today, he was excited to learn about the next pattern and the lessons it embodied.

Master Lee called the class to order, his voice calm and authoritative. "Today, we will study the seventeenth pattern: Yoo Sin. This pattern is named after General Kim Yoo Sin, one of Korea's greatest military leaders from the Silla Dynasty. He played a crucial role in unifying the Korean Peninsula under the Silla kingdom. Yoo Sin's bravery, strategic brilliance, and unwavering loyalty are the core themes of this pattern."

Sam watched intently as Master Lee demonstrated the Yoo Sin pattern. Each movement was sharp and commanding, reflecting the tactical genius and indomitable spirit of General Kim Yoo Sin. Sam followed along, striving to embody the courage and loyalty that each motion demanded.

After class, Master Lee approached Sam with a thoughtful expression. "Sam, could you help me retrieve a historical record from the library? It's an account of General Kim Yoo Sin's military campaigns, stored in the back."

Sam nodded eagerly and made his way to the library, a quiet room filled with rows of ancient books and manuscripts. As he searched through the shelves, his eyes fell upon the ancient belt, neatly folded on a high shelf. He reached for it, feeling the familiar surge of anticipation.

The moment his fingers touched the belt, the world around him dissolved into a swirl of colours. When the spinning stopped, Sam found himself standing in a vast battlefield, surrounded by soldiers in traditional Korean armour. The air was thick with the tension of an impending battle.

"Welcome, Sam," the old man's voice greeted him. Turning, Sam saw his wise guide standing beside him, a serene smile on his face.

"Where are we now?" Sam asked, taking in the intense surroundings.

"This is the site of one of General Kim Yoo Sin's significant battles during the unification wars," the old man explained. "You are here to learn about Yoo Sin, a legendary figure whose bravery and strategic brilliance helped unify Korea under the Silla Dynasty. Yoo Sin represents the ideals of courage, loyalty, and tactical mastery."

As the old man spoke, the scene shifted, and Sam found himself in a grand military camp. A tall, imposing figure stood at the centre, surrounded by his officers. Sam recognized him as General Kim Yoo Sin, a man whose presence commanded respect and loyalty from his troops.

"General Kim Yoo Sin was known for his unwavering loyalty to his king and his country," the old man continued. "He led his troops with exceptional strategic acumen, turning the tide of many battles in favour of the Silla kingdom. His leadership and bravery were instrumental in the eventual unification of the Korean Peninsula."

The scene changed again, and Sam saw Kim Yoo Sin leading his troops into a fierce battle. Despite the overwhelming enemy forces, his tactical brilliance and indomitable spirit shone through. His soldiers fought with extraordinary bravery, inspired by their leader's unwavering resolve.

"Kim Yoo Sin's loyalty was not just to his king, but also to the ideal of a unified and strong Korea," the old man said. "He understood that true strength came from unity and worked tirelessly to achieve it, even at great personal risk. His dedication to his mission and his strategic prowess are remembered as hallmarks of his legacy."

As Sam absorbed these lessons, he felt a deep respect for Kim Yoo Sin's legacy. He realized that the pattern Yoo Sin in Taekwondo was more than a series of movements; it was a tribute to a man who embodied the ideals of bravery, loyalty, and strategic mastery.

The old man placed a hand on Sam's shoulder. "Remember, Sam, the true strength of Taekwondo lies not only in physical prowess but in the bravery and loyalty you cultivate within yourself. Yoo Sin's story teaches us the importance of strategic thinking, unwavering dedication to our goals, and the courage to face any challenge."

The world around Sam began to blur once more, and he felt the familiar pull back to the present. When he opened his eyes, he was back in the library, the ancient belt still in his hand.

Master Lee's voice called out from the doorway. "Did you find the record, Sam?"

Quickly, Sam located the historical account of General Kim Yoo Sin's military campaigns and handed it to Master Lee. "Thank you, Sam. You seem to be gaining a deeper understanding of the patterns with each lesson."

As Sam left the dojang, he felt a profound sense of inspiration. He understood now that each Taekwondo pattern was not only a physical exercise but a journey into the depths of history and philosophy. With every lesson, he was not only learning the art of Taekwondo but also the values and principles that came with it.

Walking home, Sam felt a renewed sense of purpose. He was eager to continue his journey, to learn more about the legends and teachings behind each pattern, and to embody the values they represented in his own life. The story of General Kim Yoo Sin had taught him that true strength and heroism came from the virtues of bravery, loyalty, and strategic thinking. These lessons would guide him both in and out of the dojang, shaping his path as a martial artist and a person.

Chapter 18: The Legacy of Choi Yong

Choi Yong is named after General Choi Yong, Premier and Commander-in-Chief of the Armed forces during the 14th century Koryo Dynasty. Choi Yong was greatly respected for his loyalty, patriotism, and humility. He was executed by his subordinate commanders headed by General Yi Sung Gae, who later become the first king of the Lee Dynasty.

46 Movements

The dojang was filled with the rhythmic sounds of practice as Sam arrived for his next Taekwondo lesson. Each class had revealed the profound stories behind the patterns, deepening his appreciation for Taekwondo's rich heritage. Today, Sam was eager to learn about the next pattern and the lessons it held.

Master Lee called the class to order, his voice steady and authoritative. "Today, we will study the seventeenth pattern: Choi Yong. This pattern is named after General Choi Yong, a prominent military leader during the late Goryeo Dynasty. Known for his loyalty, wisdom, and martial prowess, General Choi Yong's legacy is a testament to his dedication to his country and his people."

Sam watched attentively as Master Lee demonstrated the Choi Yong pattern. Each movement was precise and powerful, reflecting the disciplined and strategic mind of General Choi Yong. Sam followed along, striving to embody the wisdom and loyalty that each motion represented.

After class, Master Lee approached Sam with a thoughtful expression. "Sam, could you help me retrieve a historical manuscript from the library? It's an account of General Choi Yong's life and contributions, stored in the back."

Sam nodded eagerly and made his way to the library, a quiet room filled with rows of ancient books and manuscripts. As he searched through the shelves, his eyes fell upon the ancient belt, neatly folded on a high shelf. He reached for it, feeling the familiar surge of anticipation.

The moment his fingers touched the belt, the world around him dissolved into a swirl of colours. When the spinning stopped, Sam found himself standing in a grand hall, surrounded by soldiers and scholars. The air was filled with the scent of ink and the murmur of strategic discussions.

"Welcome, Sam," the old man's voice greeted him. Turning, Sam saw his wise guide standing beside him, a serene smile on his face.

"Where are we now?" Sam asked, taking in the impressive surroundings.

"This is the royal court of the Goryeo Dynasty," the old man explained. "You are here to learn about General Choi Yong, a revered military leader and strategist. His loyalty to the king and his strategic brilliance made him a key figure in the defence and administration of the kingdom. Choi Yong's legacy is one of wisdom, loyalty, and unwavering dedication."

As the old man spoke, the scene shifted, and Sam found himself in the midst of a military strategy session. At the centre of the discussion was General Choi Yong, a figure of calm authority and insightful leadership. His presence commanded respect and his strategic acumen was evident in every word he spoke.

"General Choi Yong was known for his unwavering loyalty to King Gongmin and his country," the old man continued. "He played a crucial role in defending the kingdom against internal and external threats. His wisdom and martial skills earned him the respect of both his peers and his enemies."

The scene changed again, and Sam saw Choi Yong leading his troops into battle. Despite facing overwhelming odds, his strategic brilliance and disciplined leadership turned the tide of the conflict in favour of the Goryeo forces. His soldiers fought with extraordinary bravery, inspired by their leader's unwavering resolve and tactical genius.

"Choi Yong's loyalty was tested many times," the old man said. "Despite political intrigue and betrayal, he remained steadfast in his commitment to the king and the kingdom. His dedication to duty and his strategic mind were instrumental in maintaining the stability of the Goryeo Dynasty during tumultuous times."

As Sam absorbed these lessons, he felt a deep respect for Choi Yong's legacy. He realized that the pattern Choi Yong in Taekwondo was more than a series of movements; it was a tribute to a man who embodied the ideals of wisdom, loyalty, and strategic brilliance.

The old man placed a hand on Sam's shoulder. "Remember, Sam, the true strength of Taekwondo lies not only in physical prowess but in the wisdom and loyalty you cultivate within yourself. Choi Yong's story teaches us the importance of strategic thinking, unwavering dedication to our principles, and the courage to face challenges with wisdom and integrity."

The world around Sam began to blur once more, and he felt the familiar pull back to the present. When he opened his eyes, he was back in the library, the ancient belt still in his hand.

Master Lee's voice called out from the doorway. "Did you find the manuscript, Sam?"

Quickly, Sam located the historical account of General Choi Yong's life and contributions and handed it to Master Lee. "Thank you, Sam. You seem to be gaining a deeper understanding of the patterns with each lesson."

As Sam left the dojang, he felt a profound sense of inspiration. He understood now that each Taekwondo pattern was not only a physical exercise but a journey into the depths of history and philosophy. With every lesson, he was not only learning the art of Taekwondo but also the values and principles that came with it.

Walking home, Sam felt a renewed sense of purpose. He was eager to continue his journey, to learn more about the legends and teachings behind each pattern, and to embody the values they represented in his own life. The story of General Choi Yong had taught him that true strength and heroism came from the virtues of wisdom, loyalty, and strategic thinking. These lessons would guide him both in and out of the dojang, shaping his path as a martial artist and a person.

Chapter 19: The Valour of Yon Gae

Yon Gae is named after a famous general during the Koguryo Dynasty, Yon Gae Somoon. The 49 movements refer to the last two figures of 649 A. D., the Year he forced the Tang Dynasty to quit Korea after destroying nearly 300,000 of their troops at Ansi Sung.

49 Movements

The dojang was alive with the sounds of focused training as Sam arrived for his next Taekwondo lesson. Each class had illuminated the rich tapestry of Korean history through the stories behind the patterns. Today, Sam was eager to discover the next chapter in his Taekwondo journey.

Master Lee called the class to order, his voice resonating with authority. "Today, we will study the eighteenth pattern: Yon Gae. This pattern is named after General Yon Gae Somun, a formidable military leader during the Goguryeo Dynasty. Known for his fierce resistance against foreign invasions, Yon Gae Somun's legacy is a testament to his valour and strategic brilliance."

Sam watched intently as Master Lee demonstrated the Yon Gae pattern. Each movement was powerful and deliberate, reflecting the strength and determination of General Yon Gae

Somun. Sam followed along, striving to embody the valour and tactical acumen that each motion demanded.

After class, Master Lee approached Sam with a thoughtful expression. "Sam, could you help me retrieve a historical account from the library? It's a detailed chronicle of General Yon Gae Somun's campaigns, stored in the back."

Sam nodded eagerly and made his way to the library, a quiet room filled with rows of ancient books and manuscripts. As he searched through the shelves, his eyes fell upon the ancient belt, neatly folded on a high shelf. He reached for it, feeling the familiar surge of anticipation.

The moment his fingers touched the belt, the world around him dissolved into a swirl of colours. When the spinning stopped, Sam found himself standing in a fortified military camp, surrounded by soldiers preparing for battle. The air was thick with the anticipation of conflict.

"Welcome, Sam," the old man's voice greeted him. Turning, Sam saw his wise guide standing beside him, a serene smile on his face.

"Where are we now?" Sam asked, taking in the bustling surroundings.

"This is the military camp of General Yon Gae Somun," the old man explained. "You are here to learn about a legendary figure whose unyielding spirit and strategic brilliance helped defend the Goguryeo Kingdom against numerous invasions. Yon Gae Somun's legacy is one of valour, resilience, and unwavering determination."

As the old man spoke, the scene shifted, and Sam found himself in the midst of a strategic council. At the centre was General Yon Gae Somun, a commanding presence who exuded authority and confidence. His keen eyes scanned the maps and his voice carried a tone of unshakable resolve.

"General Yon Gae Somun was known for his fierce resistance against the Tang Dynasty's invasions," the old man continued. "He led his troops with unparalleled strategic insight and unyielding bravery, turning the tide of many battles in favour of the Goguryeo Kingdom. His leadership and valour were instrumental in defending the kingdom from external threats."

The scene changed again, and Sam saw Yon Gae Somun leading his troops into a fierce battle. Despite facing overwhelming odds, his tactical brilliance and unrelenting spirit inspired his soldiers to fight with extraordinary courage. The battlefield echoed with the sounds of determination and defiance.

"Yon Gae Somun's valour was not only in his martial prowess but also in his unwavering commitment to his homeland," the old man said. "He understood that the strength of a nation lay in the bravery and resilience of its people. His leadership was marked by his ability to inspire and rally his troops, even in the face of daunting challenges."

As Sam absorbed these lessons, he felt a deep respect for Yon Gae Somun's legacy. He realized that the pattern Yon Gae in Taekwondo was more than a series of movements; it was a tribute to a man who embodied the ideals of valour, resilience, and strategic brilliance.

The old man placed a hand on Sam's shoulder. "Remember, Sam, the true strength of Taekwondo lies not only in physical prowess but in the valour and resilience you cultivate within yourself. Yon Gae Somun's story teaches us the importance of unwavering determination, strategic thinking, and the courage to face any challenge head-on."

The world around Sam began to blur once more, and he felt the familiar pull back to the present. When he opened his eyes, he was back in the library, the ancient belt still in his hand.

Master Lee's voice called out from the doorway. "Did you find the chronicle, Sam?"

Quickly, Sam located the historical account of General Yon Gae Somun's campaigns and handed it to Master Lee. "Thank you, Sam. You seem to be gaining a deeper understanding of the patterns with each lesson."

As Sam left the dojang, he felt a profound sense of inspiration. He understood now that each Taekwondo pattern was not only a physical exercise but a journey into the depths of history and philosophy. With every lesson, he was not only learning the art of Taekwondo but also the values and principles that came with it.

Walking home, Sam felt a renewed sense of purpose. He was eager to continue his journey, to learn more about the legends and teachings behind each pattern, and to embody the values they represented in his own life. The story of General Yon Gae Somun had taught him that true strength and heroism came from the virtues of valour, resilience, and strategic thinking. These lessons would guide him both in and out of the dojang, shaping his path as a martial artist and a person.

Chapter 20: The Strategic Genius of Ul Ji

Ul Ji is named after general Ul-Ji Moon Dok who successfully defended Korea against a Tang's invasion force of nearly one million soldiers led by Yang Je in 612 A.D., Ul-Ji employing hit and run guerilla tactics, was able to decimate a large percentage of the force. The diagram (L) represents his surname. The 42 movements represents the author's age when he designed the pattern.

42 Movements

The dojang hummed with the disciplined energy of students as Sam arrived for his next Taekwondo lesson. Each class had taken him deeper into the heart of Korean history, revealing the rich stories behind the patterns. Today, Sam was excited to learn about the next chapter in his Taekwondo journey.

Master Lee called the class to order, his voice firm and inspiring. "Today, we will study the nineteenth pattern: Ul Ji. This pattern is named after General Ul Ji Mun Dok, a celebrated military leader from the Goguryeo Dynasty. Known for his strategic brilliance and his legendary defence against the Sui Dynasty's invasion, Ul Ji Mun Dok's legacy is a testament to his tactical genius and unwavering courage."

Sam watched closely as Master Lee demonstrated the Ul Ji pattern. Each movement was calculated and precise, reflecting the strategic mind and resolute spirit of General Ul Ji Mun Dok. Sam followed along, striving to embody the intelligence and determination that each motion represented.

After class, Master Lee approached Sam with a thoughtful expression. "Sam, could you help me retrieve a historical scroll from the library? It's an account of General Ul Ji Mun Dok's campaigns, stored in the back."

Sam nodded eagerly and made his way to the library, a quiet room filled with rows of ancient books and manuscripts. As he searched through the shelves, his eyes fell upon the ancient belt, neatly folded on a high shelf. He reached for it, feeling the familiar surge of anticipation.

The moment his fingers touched the belt, the world around him dissolved into a swirl of colours. When the spinning stopped, Sam found himself standing on a rugged battlefield, surrounded by soldiers in traditional Korean armour. The air was charged with the tension of an impending confrontation.

"Welcome, Sam," the old man's voice greeted him. Turning, Sam saw his wise guide standing beside him, a serene smile on his face.

"Where are we now?" Sam asked, taking in the intense surroundings.

"This is the site of General Ul Ji Mun Dok's legendary defense against the Sui Dynasty's invasion," the old man explained. "You are here to learn about a military genius whose strategic acumen and unwavering courage saved the Goguryeo Kingdom from a massive invading force. Ul Ji Mun Dok's legacy is one of tactical brilliance and resolute determination."

As the old man spoke, the scene shifted, and Sam found himself in a command tent. At the centre was General Ul Ji Mun Dok, a figure of calm authority and sharp intellect. His keen eyes scanned the maps, and his voice carried a tone of strategic confidence.

"General Ul Ji Mun Dok was renowned for his ability to outthink and outmanoeuvre his enemies," the old man continued. "During the Sui Dynasty's invasion, he used his deep understanding of terrain and military tactics to lead the vastly outnumbered Goguryeo forces to victory. His strategic brilliance turned the tide of the war in favour of his homeland."

The scene changed again, and Sam saw Ul Ji Mun Dok leading his troops through a series of calculated manoeuvres. Despite facing overwhelming odds, his tactical genius and unyielding spirit inspired his soldiers to fight with extraordinary resolve. The battlefield was a testament to his strategic mind and fearless leadership.

"Ul Ji Mun Dok's victory over the Sui invaders is one of the most celebrated military feats in Korean history," the old man said. "His ability to use guerrilla tactics, psychological warfare, and terrain advantage allowed him to decimate the Sui forces, despite their numerical superiority. His legacy is a powerful reminder of the impact of strategic thinking and unwavering resolve."

As Sam absorbed these lessons, he felt a deep respect for Ul Ji Mun Dok's legacy. He realized that the pattern Ul Ji in Taekwondo was more than a series of movements; it was a tribute to a man who embodied the ideals of strategic brilliance, courage, and determination.

The old man placed a hand on Sam's shoulder. "Remember, Sam, the true strength of Taekwondo lies not only in physical prowess but in the strategic thinking and determination you cultivate within yourself. Ul Ji Mun Dok's story teaches us the importance of intelligent planning, unwavering resolve, and the courage to face overwhelming challenges."

The world around Sam began to blur once more, and he felt the familiar pull back to the present. When he opened his eyes, he was back in the library, the ancient belt still in his hand.

Master Lee's voice called out from the doorway. "Did you find the scroll, Sam?"

Quickly, Sam located the historical account of General Ul Ji Mun Dok's campaigns and handed it to Master Lee. "Thank you, Sam. You seem to be gaining a deeper understanding of the patterns with each lesson."

As Sam left the dojang, he felt a profound sense of inspiration. He understood now that each Taekwondo pattern was not only a physical exercise but a journey into the depths of history and philosophy. With every lesson, he was not only learning the art of Taekwondo but also the values and principles that came with it.

Walking home, Sam felt a renewed sense of purpose. He was eager to continue his journey, to learn more about the legends and teachings behind each pattern, and to embody the values they represented in his own life. The story of General Ul Ji Mun Dok had taught him that true strength and heroism came from the virtues of strategic brilliance, courage, and unwavering resolve. These lessons would guide him both in and out of the dojang, shaping his path as a martial artist and a person.

Chapter 21: The Wisdom of Moon Moo

Moon Moo honours the 30th king of the Silla Dynasty. His body was buried near Dae Wang Am (Great King's Rock). According to his will, the body was placed in the sea "Where my soul shall forever defend my land against the Japanese." It is said that the Sok Gul Am (Stone Cave) was built to guard his tomb. The Sok Gul Am is a fine example of the culture of the Silla Dynasty. The 61 movements in this pattern symbolize the last two figures of 661 A.D. when Moon Moo came to the throne.

61 Movements

The dojang was alive with the energy of practice as Sam arrived for his next Taekwondo lesson. Each class had taken him deeper into the historical and philosophical roots of Taekwondo, revealing the stories behind the patterns. Today, Sam was eager to learn about the next chapter in his journey.

Master Lee called the class to order, his voice firm and resonant. "Today, we will study the twentieth pattern: Moon Moo. This pattern is named after King Munmu, the 30th ruler of the Silla Dynasty, who played a significant role in unifying the Korean peninsula. Known for his wisdom and strategic vision, King Munmu's legacy is a testament to his dedication to peace and unity."

Sam watched closely as Master Lee demonstrated the Moon Moo pattern. Each movement was fluid and purposeful, reflecting the wisdom and foresight of King Munmu. Sam followed along, striving to embody the intelligence and determination that each motion represented.

After class, Master Lee approached Sam with a thoughtful expression. "Sam, could you help me retrieve a historical manuscript from the library? It's an account of King Munmu's reign and his contributions to the unification of Korea, stored in the back."

Sam nodded eagerly and made his way to the library, a quiet room filled with rows of ancient books and manuscripts. As he searched through the shelves, his eyes fell upon the ancient belt, neatly folded on a high shelf. He reached for it, feeling the familiar surge of anticipation.

The moment his fingers touched the belt, the world around him dissolved into a swirl of colours. When the spinning stopped, Sam found himself standing in a grand hall, surrounded by courtiers and advisors. The air was filled with the scent of ink and the murmur of strategic discussions.

"Welcome, Sam," the old man's voice greeted him. Turning, Sam saw his wise guide standing beside him, a serene smile on his face.

101

"Where are we now?" Sam asked, taking in the impressive surroundings.

"This is the royal court of the Silla Dynasty," the old man explained. "You are here to learn about King Munmu, a ruler whose wisdom and strategic vision helped unify the Korean peninsula. His legacy is one of peace, unity, and enlightened leadership."

As the old man spoke, the scene shifted, and Sam found himself in the midst of a strategic council. At the centre was King Munmu, a figure of calm authority and deep insight. His presence commanded respect, and his strategic acumen was evident in every word he spoke.

"King Munmu was known for his ability to unite the Korean peninsula," the old man continued. "He achieved this through a combination of military strategy, diplomatic skill, and a deep commitment to peace. His reign marked the beginning of a unified Korea, a legacy that endures to this day."

The scene changed again, and Sam saw King Munmu overseeing the construction of fortifications and the organization of his army. Despite facing numerous challenges, his strategic brilliance and unyielding spirit inspired his people to work towards a common goal. The kingdom thrived under his wise and capable leadership.

"King Munmu's legacy is not only one of military achievement but also of cultural and political unity," the old man said. "He understood that true strength came from the unity of his people and the wisdom to lead them towards a prosperous future. His reign was marked by peace and stability, as he focused on consolidating his gains and fostering a sense of national identity."

As Sam absorbed these lessons, he felt a deep respect for King Munmu's legacy. He realized that the pattern Moon Moo in Taekwondo was more than a series of movements; it was a tribute to a man who embodied the ideals of wisdom, unity, and strategic vision.

The old man placed a hand on Sam's shoulder. "Remember, Sam, the true strength of Taekwondo lies not only in physical prowess but in the wisdom and unity you cultivate within yourself. King Munmu's story teaches us the importance of strategic thinking, enlightened leadership, and the pursuit of peace and unity."

The world around Sam began to blur once more, and he felt the familiar pull back to the present. When he opened his eyes, he was back in the library, the ancient belt still in his hand.

Master Lee's voice called out from the doorway. "Did you find the manuscript, Sam?"

Quickly, Sam located the historical account of King Munmu's reign and handed it to Master Lee. "Thank you, Sam. You seem to be gaining a deeper understanding of the patterns with each lesson."

As Sam left the dojang, he felt a profound sense of inspiration. He understood now that each Taekwondo pattern was not only a physical exercise but a journey into the depths of history and philosophy. With every lesson, he was not only learning the art of Taekwondo but also the values and principles that came with it.

Walking home, Sam felt a renewed sense of purpose. He was eager to continue his journey, to learn more about the legends and teachings behind each pattern, and to embody the values they represented in his own life. The story of King Munmu had taught him that true strength and heroism came from the virtues of wisdom, unity, and strategic vision. These lessons would guide him both in and out of the dojang, shaping his path as a martial artist and a person.

Chapter 22: The Endurance of So San

So San is the pseudonym of the great monk Choi Hyong Ung (1520-1604) during the Lee Dynasty. The 72 movements refer to his age when he organized a corps of monk soldiers with the assistance of his pupil Sa Myung Dang. The monk soldiers helped repulse the Japanese pirates who overran most of the Korean peninsula in 1592.

72 Movements

The dojang buzzed with energy as Sam arrived for his next Taekwondo lesson. Each class had deepened his appreciation for the historical and philosophical roots of Taekwondo, revealing the rich stories behind the patterns. Today, Sam was eager to learn about the next chapter in his journey.

Master Lee called the class to order, his voice clear and commanding. "Today, we will study the twenty-first pattern: So San. This pattern is named after Choi Hyong Ung, also known as the monk So San, a revered figure in Korean history. Known for his spiritual endurance and leadership during the Japanese invasions of Korea in the late 16th century, So San's legacy is a testament to his resilience and unwavering commitment to his country."

Sam watched closely as Master Lee demonstrated the So San pattern. Each movement was steady and deliberate, reflecting the spiritual strength and determination of the monk So San. Sam followed along, striving to embody the endurance and resilience that each motion represented.

After class, Master Lee approached Sam with a thoughtful expression. "Sam, could you help me retrieve a historical manuscript from the library? It's an account of So San's leadership during the Japanese invasions, stored in the back."

Sam nodded eagerly and made his way to the library, a quiet room filled with rows of ancient books and manuscripts. As he searched through the shelves, his eyes fell upon the ancient belt, neatly folded on a high shelf. He reached for it, feeling the familiar surge of anticipation.

The moment his fingers touched the belt, the world around him dissolved into a swirl of colours. When the spinning stopped, Sam found himself standing in a serene temple courtyard, surrounded by monks in simple robes. The air was filled with the sound of chanting and the scent of incense.

"Welcome, Sam," the old man's voice greeted him. Turning, Sam saw his wise guide standing beside him, a serene smile on his face.

"Where are we now?" Sam asked, taking in the peaceful surroundings.

"This is the Seon (Zen) temple where So San resided," the old man explained. "You are here to learn about a spiritual leader whose resilience and dedication helped defend Korea during the Japanese invasions. So San's legacy is one of spiritual endurance, strategic leadership, and unwavering commitment."

As the old man spoke, the scene shifted, and Sam found himself in a secluded meditation hall. At the centre was So San, a figure of calm authority and deep spiritual strength. His presence exuded tranquility and determination, qualities that had made him a revered leader during times of crisis.

"So San was not only a spiritual leader but also a strategic thinker," the old man continued. "During the Japanese invasions, he organized a militia of monks known as the Righteous Army, who played a crucial role in defending the country. His leadership and resilience inspired his followers to endure and resist in the face of overwhelming odds."

The scene changed again, and Sam saw So San leading his monks through rigorous training and strategic planning. Despite the chaos and destruction brought by the invasions, his spiritual strength and unyielding spirit inspired his followers to fight with extraordinary resolve. The temple became a symbol of resilience and hope.

"So San's legacy is a powerful reminder of the strength that comes from spiritual endurance and unwavering commitment to a just cause," the old man said. "He taught his followers the importance of inner strength, strategic thinking, and resilience in the face of adversity. His leadership during one of Korea's darkest times is a testament to his remarkable character."

As Sam absorbed these lessons, he felt a deep respect for So San's legacy. He realized that the pattern So San in Taekwondo was more than a series of movements; it was a tribute to a man who embodied the ideals of spiritual strength, resilience, and strategic leadership.

The old man placed a hand on Sam's shoulder. "Remember, Sam, the true strength of Taekwondo lies not only in physical prowess but in the spiritual endurance and resilience you cultivate within yourself. So San's story teaches us the importance of inner strength, strategic leadership, and the courage to face overwhelming challenges with unwavering resolve."

The world around Sam began to blur once more, and he felt the familiar pull back to the present. When he opened his eyes, he was back in the library, the ancient belt still in his hand.

Master Lee's voice called out from the doorway. "Did you find the manuscript, Sam?"

Quickly, Sam located the historical account of So San's leadership and handed it to Master Lee. "Thank you, Sam. You seem to be gaining a deeper understanding of the patterns with each lesson."

As Sam left the dojang, he felt a profound sense of inspiration. He understood now that each Taekwondo pattern was not only a physical exercise but a journey into the depths of history and philosophy. With every lesson, he was not only learning the art of Taekwondo but also the values and principles that came with it.

Walking home, Sam felt a renewed sense of purpose. He was eager to continue his journey, to learn more about the legends and teachings behind each pattern, and to embody the values they represented in his own life. The story of So San had taught him that true strength and heroism came from the virtues of spiritual endurance, resilience, and strategic leadership. These lessons would guide him both in and out of the dojang, shaping his path as a martial artist and a person.

Chapter 23: The Enlightened Reign of Se Jong

Se Jong is named after the greatest Korean king, Se-Jong, who invented the Korean alphabet in 1443, and was also a noted meteorologist. The diagram (Z) represents the king, while the 24 movements refer to the 24 letters of the Korean alphabet.

24 Movements

The dojang was a hive of activity as Sam arrived for his next Taekwondo lesson. Each class had revealed more about the historical and philosophical roots of Taekwondo, enriching his understanding of the patterns. Today, Sam was eager to delve into the next chapter of his journey.

Master Lee called the class to attention, his voice resonant and authoritative. "Today, we will study the twenty-third pattern: Se Jong. This pattern is named after King Sejong the Great, the fourth king of the Joseon Dynasty. Known for his enlightened rule and cultural contributions, King Sejong's legacy is a testament to his wisdom, innovation, and dedication to the welfare of his people."

Sam watched intently as Master Lee demonstrated the Se Jong pattern. Each movement was graceful and purposeful, reflecting the enlightened mind and visionary leadership of King Sejong. Sam followed along, striving to embody the wisdom and innovation that each motion represented.

After class, Master Lee approached Sam with a thoughtful expression. "Sam, could you help me retrieve a historical manuscript from the library? It's an account of King Sejong's reign and his contributions to Korean culture, stored in the back."

Sam nodded eagerly and made his way to the library, a quiet room filled with rows of ancient books and manuscripts. As he searched through the shelves, his eyes fell upon the ancient belt, neatly folded on a high shelf. He reached for it, feeling the familiar surge of anticipation.

The moment his fingers touched the belt, the world around him dissolved into a swirl of colours. When the spinning stopped, Sam found himself standing in a grand hall, surrounded by scholars and courtiers. The air was filled with the hum of intellectual discourse and the scent of ink and parchment.

"Welcome, Sam," the old man's voice greeted him. Turning, Sam saw his wise guide standing beside him, a serene smile on his face.

"Where are we now?" Sam asked, taking in the impressive surroundings.

"This is the royal court of the Joseon Dynasty," the old man explained. "You are here to learn about King Sejong the Great, a ruler whose enlightened leadership and innovative spirit left an indelible mark on Korean history. Sejong's legacy is one of wisdom, cultural advancement, and deep commitment to the welfare of his people."

As the old man spoke, the scene shifted, and Sam found himself in the midst of a scholarly gathering. At the centre was King Sejong, a figure of calm authority and intellectual vigour. His presence exuded wisdom and vision, qualities that had made him one of Korea's most revered monarchs.

"King Sejong was known for his profound contributions to Korean culture and society," the old man continued. "He championed education, science, and technology, and his creation of the Korean script, Hangul, revolutionized literacy and communication in Korea. His reign was marked by a deep commitment to the enlightenment and prosperity of his people."

The scene changed again, and Sam saw King Sejong overseeing the development of Hangul with a group of scholars. Despite the challenges and opposition he faced, his innovative spirit and unwavering determination led to the creation of a writing system that was easy to learn and accessible to all Koreans. This revolutionary achievement fostered widespread literacy and cultural growth.

"King Sejong's legacy is a powerful reminder of the impact of enlightened leadership and innovation," the old man said. "His contributions to science, technology, and the arts laid the foundation for Korea's cultural and intellectual advancement. His vision and dedication to his people's welfare made him a beloved and respected ruler."

As Sam absorbed these lessons, he felt a deep respect for King Sejong's legacy. He realized that the pattern Se Jong in Taekwondo was more than a series of movements; it was a tribute to a man who embodied the ideals of wisdom, innovation, and enlightened leadership.

The old man placed a hand on Sam's shoulder. "Remember, Sam, the true strength of Taekwondo lies not only in physical prowess but in the wisdom and innovation you cultivate within yourself. King Sejong's story teaches us the importance of intellectual growth, cultural advancement, and the commitment to improving the lives of others."

The world around Sam began to blur once more, and he felt the familiar pull back to the present. When he opened his eyes, he was back in the library, the ancient belt still in his hand.

Master Lee's voice called out from the doorway. "Did you find the manuscript, Sam?"

Quickly, Sam located the historical account of King Sejong's reign and handed it to Master Lee. "Thank you, Sam. You seem to be gaining a deeper understanding of the patterns with each lesson."

As Sam left the dojang, he felt a profound sense of inspiration. He understood now that each Taekwondo pattern was not only a physical exercise but a journey into the depths of history and philosophy. With every lesson, he was not only learning the art of Taekwondo but also the values and principles that came with it.

Walking home, Sam felt a renewed sense of purpose. He was eager to continue his journey, to learn more about the legends and teachings behind each pattern, and to embody the values they represented in his own life. The story of King Sejong had taught him that true strength and heroism came from the virtues of wisdom, innovation, and enlightened leadership. These lessons would guide him both in and out of the dojang, shaping his path as a martial artist and a person.

Chapter 24: The Unity of Tong Il

---

*Tong Il denotes the resolution of the
unification of Korea which has been divided
since 1945. The diagram (|) symbolizes the
homogenous race.*

56 Movements

The dojang was bustling with anticipation as Sam arrived for his next Taekwondo lesson. Each class had further enriched his understanding of Taekwondo's historical and philosophical roots, and today he was eager to delve into the next chapter of his journey.

Master Lee called the class to attention, his voice firm and inspiring. "Today, we will study the twenty-fourth pattern: Tong Il. This pattern symbolizes the unification of Korea and the hope for a peaceful future. The term 'Tong Il' means 'unification' in Korean, reflecting the aspiration for unity and harmony."

Sam watched intently as Master Lee demonstrated the Tong Il pattern. Each movement was deliberate and harmonious, embodying the spirit of unity and the hope for peace. Sam followed along, striving to embody the ideals of harmony and unification that each motion represented.

After class, Master Lee approached Sam with a thoughtful expression. "Sam, could you help me retrieve a historical document from the library? It's a treatise on the concept of Tong Il and its significance in Korean history, stored in the back."

Sam nodded eagerly and made his way to the library, a quiet room filled with rows of ancient books and manuscripts. As he searched through the shelves, his eyes fell upon the ancient belt, neatly folded on a high shelf. He reached for it, feeling the familiar surge of anticipation.

The moment his fingers touched the belt, the world around him dissolved into a swirl of colours. When the spinning stopped, Sam found himself standing in a serene garden, surrounded by symbols of unity and peace. The air was filled with the scent of blooming flowers and the gentle sound of flowing water.

"Welcome, Sam," the old man's voice greeted him. Turning, Sam saw his wise guide standing beside him, a serene smile on his face.

"Where are we now?" Sam asked, taking in the peaceful surroundings.

"This is a symbolic representation of the ideal of Tong Il," the old man explained. "You are here to learn about the profound significance of unification in Korean history and culture. Tong Il embodies the hope for a unified and peaceful Korea, a vision that has guided many leaders and inspired countless people."

As the old man spoke, the scene shifted, and Sam found himself in the midst of historical moments that highlighted the importance of unity. He saw leaders and visionaries striving to bring about harmony and reconciliation, each effort a testament to the enduring dream of Tong Il.

"Tong Il represents the aspiration for a Korea united in peace and harmony," the old man continued. "Throughout history, the concept of unification has been a guiding principle, inspiring efforts to overcome division and conflict. It is a vision of a future where all Koreans live together in mutual respect and cooperation."

The scene changed again, and Sam saw communities coming together, working towards common goals, and fostering a spirit of unity. Despite the challenges and obstacles, the collective efforts of individuals dedicated to Tong Il created a powerful momentum towards peace and reconciliation.

"The legacy of Tong Il is a reminder of the importance of unity and cooperation," the old man said. "It teaches us that true strength lies in our ability to come together, to overcome differences, and to work towards a common vision of peace and harmony. This ideal is central to the spirit of Taekwondo and the values it seeks to instil."

As Sam absorbed these lessons, he felt a deep respect for the concept of Tong Il. He realized that the pattern Tong Il in

Taekwondo was more than a series of movements; it was a tribute to the enduring aspiration for unity and peace.

The old man placed a hand on Sam's shoulder. "Remember, Sam, the true strength of Taekwondo lies not only in physical prowess but in the unity and harmony you cultivate within yourself and with others. Tong Il's story teaches us the importance of coming together, embracing our shared humanity, and working towards a peaceful future."

The world around Sam began to blur once more, and he felt the familiar pull back to the present. When he opened his eyes, he was back in the library, the ancient belt still in his hand.

Master Lee's voice called out from the doorway. "Did you find the document, Sam?"

Quickly, Sam located the treatise on Tong Il and handed it to Master Lee. "Thank you, Sam. You seem to be gaining a deeper understanding of the patterns with each lesson."

As Sam left the dojang, he felt a profound sense of inspiration. He understood now that each Taekwondo pattern was not only a physical exercise but a journey into the depths of history and philosophy. With every lesson, he was not only learning the art of Taekwondo but also the values and principles that came with it.

Walking home, Sam felt a renewed sense of purpose. He was eager to continue his journey, to learn more about the legends and teachings behind each pattern, and to embody the values they represented in his own life. The story of Tong Il had taught him that true strength and heroism came from the virtues of unity, harmony, and the shared vision of a peaceful future. These lessons would guide him both in and out of the dojang, shaping his path as a martial artist and a person.

Chapter 25: The Journey of Taekwondo

The dojang was a blend of excitement and nostalgia as Sam arrived for what he knew would be his final lesson in this transformative series. The journey through the historical and philosophical roots of Taekwondo had profoundly shaped his understanding and appreciation of the art. Today, there was a sense of culmination, a feeling that he was about to bring his journey full circle.

Master Lee called the class to attention, his voice filled with a sense of finality and pride. "Today, we conclude our journey with a reflection on all we have learned. Each pattern we have studied carries a piece of history, philosophy, and wisdom. Together, they form the foundation of Taekwondo and the principles we strive to embody."

Sam stood with his classmates, a sense of unity and accomplishment filling the room. They began with a series of warm-ups and moved into practicing the patterns they had studied so diligently. As they flowed from one pattern to the next, Sam felt a deep connection to the historical figures and events that had guided him through each movement.

After class, Master Lee approached Sam with a warm smile. "Sam, could you help me with one final task? There's a special item in the equipment cupboard that I'd like you to find."

Sam nodded eagerly and made his way to the cupboard, his heart pounding with anticipation. As he searched through the equipment, his eyes fell upon the ancient belt once more. He reached for it, feeling the familiar surge of energy.

The moment his fingers touched the belt, the world around him dissolved into a swirl of colours. When the spinning stopped, Sam found himself standing in a tranquil meadow, surrounded by the symbols and figures he had encountered throughout his journey. The air was filled with a sense of peace and completion.

"Welcome, Sam," the old man's voice greeted him. Turning, Sam saw his wise guide standing beside him, a serene smile on his face.

"Is this the end of my journey?" Sam asked, taking in the serene surroundings.

"This is a moment of reflection and understanding," the old man explained. "You have learned about the historical and philosophical roots of Taekwondo. Now, you are here to see how these lessons come together to form a cohesive whole."

As the old man spoke, the scene shifted, and Sam saw the various figures and events from his journey – from Dan Gun to

Tong Il. Each figure stood together, united in their contributions to the rich tapestry of Taekwondo's history.

"Each pattern you learned was a piece of a larger puzzle," the old man continued. "Together, they teach us about resilience, wisdom, unity, and the pursuit of peace. These lessons are not just for the dojang but for every aspect of your life."

The scene changed again, and Sam saw himself practicing Taekwondo, embodying the principles he had learned. He saw moments of struggle and triumph, times when the lessons of Taekwondo had guided him through challenges and helped him grow as a person.

"The journey of Taekwondo is never truly over," the old man said. "It is a continuous path of self-discovery, growth, and the pursuit of harmony. You have learned much, but there is always more to understand and embody."

As Sam absorbed these final lessons, he felt a deep sense of gratitude and fulfilment. He realized that his journey through Taekwondo had only just begun and that the lessons he had learned would continue to guide him throughout his life.

The old man placed a hand on Sam's shoulder. "Remember, Sam, the true essence of Taekwondo lies in the unity of mind, body, and spirit. It is in the principles of harmony, respect, and the continuous pursuit of betterment. Carry these lessons with you always."

The world around Sam began to blur once more, and he felt the familiar pull back to the present. When he opened his eyes, he was back in the dojang, the ancient belt still in his hand.

Master Lee's voice called out from the doorway. "Did you find the special item, Sam?"

Sam nodded and handed the belt to Master Lee. "Thank you, Sam. This belt represents the journey you have undertaken. It symbolizes the unity and harmony you have come to understand."

As the class gathered for a final bow, Sam felt a profound sense of completion and anticipation for the future. He knew that the journey of Taekwondo was a lifelong path, one that he was eager to continue exploring.

Walking home, Sam reflected on his journey. He had learned about legendary figures and pivotal moments in Korean history, each one teaching him valuable lessons about strength, resilience, wisdom, and unity. The stories and principles behind each pattern had shaped him into a better martial artist and person.

Sam felt a renewed sense of purpose. He was eager to continue embodying the values he had learned, both in and out of the dojang. He realized that his journey in Taekwondo was just beginning, and the lessons of the patterns would guide him throughout his life.

And so, Sam's journey through the patterns came to a close, but the lessons he had learned would stay with him forever. He understood that the true essence of Taekwondo lay in the unity of mind, body, and spirit, and in the pursuit of harmony and peace. With this knowledge, Sam felt prepared to face the future, confident in his abilities and grounded in the timeless principles of Taekwondo.

As he reached his front door, Sam paused and looked up at the sky. The journey had been transformative, and he felt grateful for the wisdom and guidance he had received. With a deep breath, he stepped inside, ready to continue his path as a martial artist and a person dedicated to the principles of Taekwondo.

The end of this chapter marked the beginning of many more. Sam knew that with every step, every practice, and every challenge, he would carry the lessons of Taekwondo within him, guiding him towards a life of balance, respect, and unending growth.

Printed in Great Britain
by Amazon